SQUADRONS!

No. 59

THE DUTCH FIGHTER SQUADRONS
- Nos 322 & 120 (NEI) Squadrons -

Phil H. Listemann

ISBN: 978-2494471-00-9

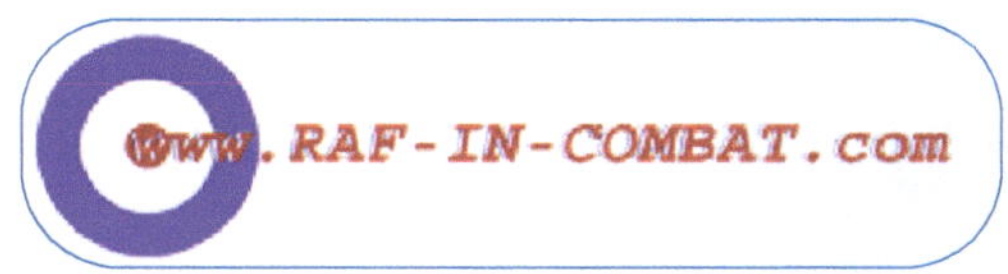

Colour profiles: Gaetan Marie/Bravo Bravo Aviation

GLOSSARY OF TERMS

PERSONEL :
(AUS)/RAF: Australian serving in the RAF
(BEL)/RAF: Belgian serving in the RAF
(CAN)/RAF: Canadian serving in the RAF
(CZ)/RAF: Czechoslovak serving in the RAF
(NFL)/RAF: Newfoundlander serving in the RAF
(NL)/RAF: Dutch serving in the RAF
(NZ)/RAF: New Zealander serving in the RAF
(POL)/RAF: Pole serving in the RAF
(RHO)/RAF: Rhodesian serving in the RAF
(SA)/RAF: South African serving in the RAF
(US)/RAF - RCAF : American serving in the RAF or RCAF

RANKS
G/C : Group Captain
W/C : Wing Commander
S/L : Squadron Leader
F/L : Flight Lieutenant
F/O : Flying Officer
P/O : Pilot Officer
W/O : Warrant Officer
F/Sgt : Flight Sergeant
Sgt : Sergeant
Cpl : Corporal
LAC : Leading Aircraftman

OTHER
ATA: Air Transport Auxiliary
CO : Commander
DFC : Distinguished Flying Cross
DFM : Distinguished Flying Medal
DSO : Distinguished Service Order
Eva. : Evaded
ORB : Operational Record Book
OTU : Operational Training Unit
PoW : Prisoner of War
PAF: Polish Air Force
RAF : Royal Air Force
RAAF : Royal Australian Air Force
RCAF : Royal Canadian Air Force
RNZAF : Royal New Zealand Air Force
SAAF : South African Air Force
s/d: Shot down
Sqn : Squadron
† : Killed

CODENAMES - OFFENSIVE OPERATIONS - FIGHTER COMMAND

CIRCUS:
Bombers heavily escorted by fighters, the purpose being to bring enemy fighters into combat.

RAMROD:
Bombers escorted by fighters, the primary aim being to destroy a target.

RANGER:
Large formation freelance intrusion over enemy territory with aim of wearing down enemy fighters.

RHUBARB:
Freelance fighter sortie against targets of opportunity.

ROADSTEAD:
Dive bombing and low level attacks on enemy ships at sea or in harbour

RODEO:
A fighter sweep without bombers.

SWEEP:
An offensive flight by fighters designed to draw up and clear the enemy from the sky.

Princess Juliana of the Netherlands visiting No. 322 (Dutch) Squadron during Summer 1944. Note the 'Netherlands' shoulder flash worn by the two pilots talking with the princess, an insignia surprisingly not worn by S/L van Eendenburg on the far right, who was OC at the time. About 40 Dutch pilots served with 322 between 1943 and 1945, while about 30 others served with various RAF fighter squadrons between 1940 and 1945 and were never posted to 322. With so few available fighter pilots, it was not possible to form more than one fighter squadron with enough reserves to allow for turnover of personnel and to cover attrition.
(*Netherlands Institute for Military History, The Hague*)

THE DUTCH FIGHTER PILOTS WITH THE ALLIES

Recruiting airmen after the Netherlands was occupied in May 1940 remained a major issue for the Dutch throughout the war. While other occupied countries managed to deliver airmen, groundcrew, and sometimes trainees, the Dutch did not. Paradoxically, as early as June 1940, they were the first to form their own squadrons within the RAF. But, while they were able to form these units (Nos. 320 and 321), it was only achieved because material and personnel, Dutch Navy personnel in this case, had been spirited away from under the noses of the Germans. That would be it for many years, though. Indeed, the Dutch Army had its own air service, and many of its personnel found asylum in Britain, but, from the start, the number of trained pilots was low as The Netherlands, in May 1940, only had a small active air force. At first the British thought they would be more useful to the Dutch colonies in the East Indies where a rather important air arm, the NEIAF (Netherlands East Indies Air Force), was well established. However, the Dutch government in exile notified the British new arrivals would remain to fight the Germans. Politics slowed the process of integration in many ways, the Dutch being split between wanting to fight the Germans (and the RAF needed any pilots it could get) and the need to reinforce the East Indies against the increasing Japanese threat. For the personnel in the UK who had family under German rule, the decision to be incorporated into the NEIAF was not an automatic one and they were largely reluctant to do so. In any case, the Dutch pilots had to be trained, or re-trained, and, when available, posted to existing RAF squadrons. There were not enough to form a full Dutch fighter unit, and no clear decision was made in 1941, so the situation remained unresolved until Java surrendered to the Japanese in March 1942. From then, the solution was simple. Some additional Dutch personnel were repatriated to Britain as they had nowhere else to go; this opened the door for the formation of a full Dutch fighter squadron. A specific Dutch unit, as with the Belgians, was initially established as a flight within an operational unit, No. 167 (Gold Coast) Squadron, which progressively formed throughout 1942. Formed in April, B Flight began to be manned by Dutch pilots from August. The squadron was busy during the year, flying about 1,550 sorties. During the year, 167 lost two Dutch pilots, Pilot Officer C. Geesink on 13 November 1942 (PoW) and Pilot Officer Coen de Iongh on 10 June 1943 (Killed in Action). Two days later, on 12 June, a Dutch fighter squadron in the RAF was finally formed. It would be the only one, No. 322. For the NEIAF, the situation would be different (see No. 120 Squadron, NEI)

Victories - confirmed or probable claims: 119.0 V-1s

First operational sortie:
17.06.43
Last operational sortie:
07.05.45

Number of sorties: *ca.*4,850

Total aircraft written-off: 40

Aircraft lost on operations: 31
Aircraft lost in accidents: 9

Squadron code letters:
VL, 3W

Commanding Officers

S/L Archibald C. Stewart	RAF No. 40151	RAF	12.06.43	01.09.43
F/L John B. Niven (*Temp.*)	RAF No. 109061	RAF	01.09.43	22.09.43
Maj Keith C. Kuhlmann (*PoW*)	SAAF No. P102441	SAAF	22.09.43	01.09.44
F/L Jan van Arkel (*Temp.*)	RAF No. 124639	(NL)/RAF	02.09.44	12.09.44
S/L Leendert van Eendenburg	RAF No. 108814	(NL)/RAF	12.09.44	17.11.44
S/L Hugh F. O'Neill	RAF No. 41312	RAF	17.11.44	02.03.45
S/L Bram van der Stok	RAF No. 106346	(NL)/RAF	02.03.45	07.10.45

SQUADRON USAGE

This unit was not a new squadron as such at is came about from the redenomination of No. 167 (Gold Coast) Squadron on 12 June 1943. Indeed, for a couple of months the squadron had had a flight manned by Dutch pilots. During the spring of 1943, it was decided to raise a full Dutch fighter squadron from the nucleus of 167. The change of denomination took place at the same time the unit moved from Westhampnett to Woodvale, near Liverpool. There was no change in organisation, with S/L A.C. Stewart remaining in command assisted by his two flight commanders, Flight Lieutenants A.R. Hall (South Africa) and M.G. Barnett (New Zealand). The latter was almost immediately re-posted to No. 485 Squadron three days later, replaced by F/L Watts. The Dutch personnel in the former 167 Squadron numbered just eight pilots gathered in B Flight: Flying Officers L. van Eendenburg, J. Plesman, and J. van Arkel, Pilot Officers J. Jonkers, E. Baron van Nagell, J. van Hamel, C. de Iongh, N. Sluyter, and Sgt J. Maier. New Dutch pilots soon arrived at the 'new' squadron however: Flying Officers L. Meijers, J. Flinterman and W. de Wolff, on 16 June, and before the end of the month they were reinforced by Flight Lieutenants J. Dekker and M. Muller, Flying Officers G. Aalpoel, G. Jongbloed, C. Manders, and Pilot Officers R. van Daalen Wetters and J. Arts. At the same time, operational activity remained low for the month with sixteen sorties carried out (mainly uneventful scrambles). In July, the turnover of pilots continued with more Dutch posted in while non-Dutch pilots were posted out. Also, F/O J. Plesman took over B Flight from F/L Watts early in the month. Operations were limited to a single patrol by two Spitfires on the 26th conducted by F/L F.D. Snalam (British) and Sgt J. Maier. In August, F/L Hall left and a Scottish pilot, F/L J.B. Niven, arrived to take over the A Flight commander's position. At the end of August, news came through that S/L Stewart would leave and be replaced by a South African, Capt. K.C. Kuhlmann (SAAF), who had received a DFC earlier in the year while serving with No. 185 Squadron in the Mediterranean. In August, the pilots were scrambled three times, but all returned with nothing to report. That was it for the month's operational activity. Flight Lieutenant Niven became the temporary CO pending the arrival of Major Kuhlmann on 22 September. Autumn 1943 was quiet and was spent mainly on training flights and exercises. However, on 11 October, from 11.00 to 14.00, the squadron put twelve Spitfires in the air to escort a DH Flamingo aircraft carrying Princess Mary to the Isle of Man. The return journey took place three days later and 322 provided ten Spitfires as escort. During that period of time, ending in December 1943, only a few incidents were reported, but none were fatal or of serious consequence. On 6 November Sgt F. van Valkenburg, who had been with the squadron since September, was unfortunate to burst a tyre on landing. The aircraft ran off the runway and tipped onto its nose. It was his second accident in about a week, having made a belly landing on 27 October after the landing gear failed. In the afternoon, Sgt G. Dirkman experienced a glycol leak that

Archibald Cathcart STEWART

RAF No. 40151

Archibald Stewart enlisted in the RAF in 1937 and started the war as a bomber pilot and was serving with No. 57 Squadron at the outbreak flying Blenheims. This unit moved to France after September 1939, but Stewart fell victim to a serious accident in April 1940. He then spent nearly two years in hospital. On recovery, he was advised to go onto single engine aircraft because his left knee was too weak to handle twin-engine aircraft, especially in the event of an engine failure. He initially served with 175 Squadron in 1942 before being posted to No. 167 (Gold Coast) Squadron in February 1943 to command, then becoming OC 322 (Dutch) Squadron when the later was formed raised from 167. He left 322 in August 1943 and took over No. 122 (Bombay) Squadron in December 1943 before becoming acting wing leader of No. 122 Airfield at the end of February 1944, then promoted wing leader of No. 125 Airfield/Wing in March 1944. He ended his tour in July. He was awarded the DFC in September 1944 and no operational position was given until the end of the war. He served in the RAF after the war and retired as an Air Commodore in 1961.

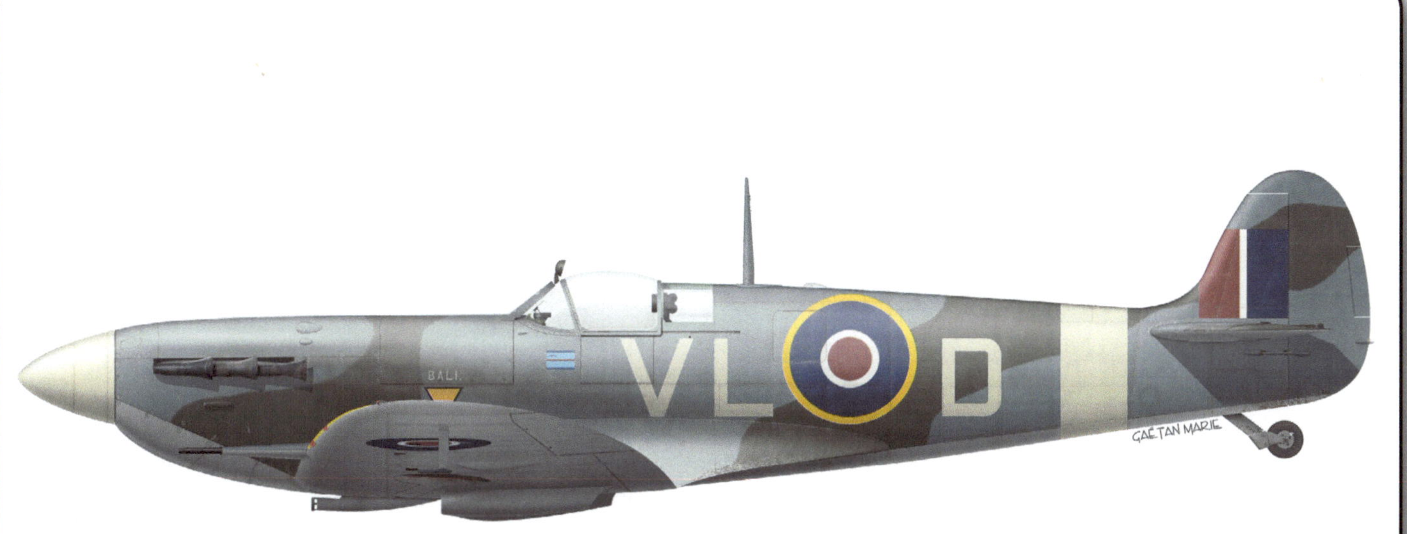

Supermarine Spitfire Mk.VB serial unknown 'Bali'
No. 322 (Dutch) Squadron
Squadron Leader A.C. Stewart
Hornchurch (UK), summer 1943

322 Sqn at Woodvale, England, in December 1943. Most of these pilots participated in the V-1 campaign a few months later:
Back row (left to right): Flight Sergeants J. Harms, C. Kooy (†28.01.45), W. Kuyper, and R. van Beers (PoW 26.08.44), P/O P. Cramerus, Flight Sergeants M. Janssen, J. Maier (†12.07.44), F. van Valkenburg, and W. de Vries, Flying Officers J. van Arkel, E. van Nagell (†28.01.44), C. Manders, and M. Muller.
Middle row (left to right): Flying Officers J. Arts and J. Flinterman, Flight Sergeants G. Dijkman and H. Roovers (†02.05.44), F/O F. van Eijk (†14.02.45), F/Sgt H. Cramm (†30.03.45), Flying Officers R. van Daalen Wetters and G. Jongbloed, F/Sgt J. van Roosendaal, Flying Officers J. van Hamel (†11.04.44), J. Jonker and L. Wolters (†16.09.44).
Front row (left to right): Flying Officers M. van Bergen, J. Dekker, and Schudel (Medical Officer), Flight Lieutenants W. de Wolff and J. Plesman, Maj. K.C. Kuhlmann (CO - SAAF) with 'Polly Grey' the mascot, Flight Lieutenants J.B. Niven (RAF), L. van Eendenburg, and L.E. Chiswell (Adj), P/O J.G. Lockton (IO), F/O L. Meyers.
(Collections Nederlands Instituut voor Militaire Historie - NIMH)

required him to make a forced landing four miles southwest of the airfield. It was the second glycol leak resulting in a forced landing as F/O G. de Neve suffered such an experience on 28 October. Early in November, some of the squadron's Spitfires were contaminated by mustard gas during an exercise, reducing the capacity of the unit. However, this was to have an almost disastrous consequence when, on 9 November, F/O van Nagell fell victim to the gas because his aircraft hadn't been decontaminated properly. He returned after ten minutes of flight, but, fortunately, with no serious issues. Sooner or later, the squadron, with so much misadventure, had to lose an aircraft and this happened on 25 November when Sgt J. van Rosendaal in AB904 taxied into Sgt M. Janssen's Spitfire, BL715. The latter was so badly damaged that it was written off. Bad weather prevented much flying in December with the first flying day being the 11th. On the 21st the squadron received notification that it was going to move south on the 30th, news that was welcomed by the personnel. The destination was Hawkinge despite Hornchurch having been mentioned previously. The squadron would take over No. 350 (Belgian) Squadron aircraft and the aircraft would continue to be serviced by the Belgian echelon.

The first day of January was not a day off as the personnel were very busy getting settled in to their quarters, dispersal and offices and repainting squadron codes on the aircraft. No flying occurred, but it resumed the next day on a small scale. The big day for the squadron came on the 4th when it carried out its first operation. Two bomber escorts, to targets located in the north of France, were the order of the day, one in the morning and one in the afternoon, both led by Major Kuhlmann. The tasking was repeated the following day, but only in the morning as the afternoon was spent flying sector recces and air tests. On 6 January, 322 was up again for a morning bomber escort. All went well, but on return F/O van Arkel was unable to get his undercarriage down and had to make a belly landing on the airfield. He escaped without injury and the Spitfire was not badly damaged. Flying Officer Meijers also pranged a Spitfire by running into a starter trolley when taxiing for take off. He was uninjured, but the aircraft was badly damaged. The squadron flew another escort on the 7th, but bad weather prevented any further ops until the 14th. That day, led by the CO, the squadron took off at 11.00 to escort 54 Marauders to military targets at Cocove and Cormette. The next day, F/L Niven scrambled at the head of five aircraft to carry out a defensive patrol. No enemy aircraft were seen and the formation returned to base after forty minutes. These would the only operational flights for the next five days, but the squadron lost its first pilot when, on the 16th, F/O G. de Neve was killed during dogfight practice with Typhoons. The 21st was a busy day for the squadron with two escort ops, one in the morning for American Marauders and one more in the afternoon for RAF Mosquitos. The squadron also flew a 'Jim Crow' sortie, led by F/L Niven, and a shipping recce led by F/L J.L. Plesman. The 23rd and 24th added another two escorts, both led by F/L

Spitfire BM354/VL-A 'Malang' seen at Llanbedr during the winter 1943-1944. This Spitfire served with 322 between July 1943 and January 1944.
(Andrew Thomas)

Niven, for Marauders and Bostons respectively, with an ASR patrol also carried out on the 24th. With bad weather, the airfield became unserviceable for a couple of days, but 322 was active again on the 28th with defensive patrols flown off Dover. Green section, F/O van Nagell and F/O Wolters, met heavy flak over the French coast after breaking through the cloud cover. The former was last seen flying in an easterly direction. He was posted missing and consequently became 322's first operational casualty. The next day, the CO led another escort for 36 Marauders, his last before relinquishing command for three weeks to F/L Niven so he could attend a course at the Fighter Leader School the next day. That same day, the 30th, F/Sgt Meier and Sgt Cramm were sent off to escort a damaged B-17 to Manston, but the Fortress finally landed four miles south of Manston in a field. The month closed with a total of 162 operational sorties.

In February, the squadron carried out fifteen bomber escorts, all but one within the first fortnight. The last was flown on the 20th and was led by the recently returned Major Kuhlmann. Poor weather was the main reason for the lack of flying for the remainder of the month. With more than 180 sorties achieved, it was a good effort nonetheless especially as no losses were recorded during this time. On the 21st the squadron was notified that it would be to detached to Ayr for a week so the aircraft could be equipped to carry bombs. At Ayr, the Dutch practiced dive-bombing and, if F/O Meijers' overshoot on the 27th (without major consequence for aircraft and pilot) is excluded, the time spent in Scotland was uneventful. The pilots returned to Hawkinge on 1 March, but only one op was flown before the squadron moved to Acklington, north of Newcastle, on the 9th where it would work closely with No. 501 Squadron. This was not the only change, however, because, two days later, F/L Plesman landed in the new type of Spitfire they would soon receive, the Mk.XIV, the second Griffon-engined variant to become operational. The days of the Spitfire V were therefore numbered, but it would be some time before the conversion was complete. It was not until 10 April that the squadron could count twenty Spitfire XIVs on hand. In the meantime, the Dutch were still flying the Mk.V and, in the first days of April, some scrambles were ordered to investigate a 'hostile plot'. The three scrambles on the 6th, 7th and 12th were uneventful. Seven days later, on the 19th, Flying Officers J. Dekker and M. van Bergen were ordered to search for a parachute seen floating 2.5 miles off Newbiggin. They orbited the position, but, after a meticulous search, only a lifeboat was found. As the visibility deteriorated from 1000 yards to 300 yards, the two Dutch pilots returned to base after more than 1.50 hours of flight. These were the last two Spitfire V operational sorties flown by the squadron to make a total of 430 since formation.

After flying the ageing Spitfire Mk.V for about nine months , it was time for the Dutch to change mounts. The latest mark, the Mk.XIV, had recently been introduced into service and the Dutch were pleased to know they would convert soon. To do so, they left Hawkinge for Ackington on 10 March under the supervision of Major K.C. Kuhlmann, the South African OC. The first Mk.XIV arrived the following day with F/L J. Plesman at the controls. The squadron, with the arrival of other aircraft, began the conversion,

On 22 September 1943 Prince Bernhard of the Netherlands visited 322 (Dutch) Squadron at Woodvale and all of the aircraft were given names in honour of the occasion. Spitfire BM515/VL-P became 'Prinses Beatrix'. Three other Spitfires were given names of the princesses: 'Prinses Iren' (BL715), 'Prinses Juliana' (AB814), and 'Prinses Margriet' (BL516).
Middle left, the nose of VL-P with the orange triangle and the new name 'Prinses Beatrix' painted on it. Below, the nose of Spitfire W3127 'Soesterberg'. It was actually the aircraft's second name after previously being called 'Celebes'.

Jan Leendert PLESMAN

RAF No. 102524

A pre-war Dutch Air Force officer, Jan Plesman fled the Netherlands in September 1940 via France, Spain and Portugal. He arrived in England in May 1941 and immediately enlisted in the RAF. Because of his flying experience, his training was shorter and, in March 1942, he joined his first operational unit, No. 64 Squadron. He remained with 64 until July 1942 when he was posted to No. 167 Squadron where a Dutch flight had been formed. This unit was raised into a full Dutch squadron, No. 322, in June 1943, and he became a flight commander soon after. Plesman distinguished himself the year after during the V-1 campaign, destroying 11 V-1s when the squadron was equipped with the Griffon-powered Spitfire Mk.XIV. In August, 322 re-equipped with the Spitfire Mk.IX and its role changed to armed recces and escorts over the Continent. On 1 September 1944, F/L Plesman led an armed recce over northern France and attacked a gun post near Lille; he was hit by flak and seen to spin into the ground. Plesman was killed in the subsequent crash.

Supermarine Spitfire Mk.VB BM515 'Prinses Beatrix'
No. 322 (Dutch) Squadron
Flight Lieutenant J. Plesman
Hornchurch (UK), autumn 1943

A 322 Sqn Spitfire V being serviced in February 1944. Most of the fighter squadrons still operating the Mk.V over the front at the time were flying aircraft with clipped wings. The last known Spitfire Vs in service with 322 were W3209, W3898,W3899, AB180, AB271, AD182, AD227, AD348, AR327, AR328, AR340, AR437, BL638, BL987, BL990, BM207, BM344, BM488, EP664.

but it was a big step from the Mk.V to the XIV. An extensive ground school, therefore, was the first step. It is not until the 17th that the first test flight was undertaken, the CO having the privilege. The two flight commanders, Flight Lieutenants Plesman and van Eendenburg, followed suit the next day. In addition to the practice flights with the Mk.XIVs, the squadron continued to fly some operations with the old Mk.Vs as previously mentioned. A drama occurred on 11 April when F/O J. van Hamel took off for an altitude test. He was seen, about 45 minutes after take off, to crash into a hillside southwest of Rothbury. While the cause of the crash was never determined, it was suspected he had experienced an oxygen failure. This, and some minor incidents, was the only major event of note before the squadron moved to 141 Airfield at Hartford Bridge with W/C Barthold as wing leader. The move took place on 23 April (RB141/L, RB158, RB160/VL-A, RB168, RB171/E, RB184/B, RB186, RB189). The next day the Dutch completed four scrambles, three to investigate unidentified aircraft and one to investigate a fighter in difficulty. The tasking for the Dutch was to prevent the Germans from taking high altitude photographs of the English coast. Unknown to the Dutch, D-Day was approaching and the extent of the preparations for the invasion had to be kept from the Germans as much as possible. The following days, more scrambles took place, but all were subsequently converted to defensive patrols. This remained the daily task for a few days. On the 27th F/O L. Wolters and F/O M. van Bergen closed on a German aircraft, but turned for home near Cherbourg while they still had enough fuel. By 30 April the squadron had already carried out about 100 standing defensive patrols (mainly over the Isle of Wight). In May, this number increased to 500, but the squadron lost two aircraft. The first loss occurred on 2 May when Sgt H. Roovers never returned from a patrol late in the evening. That evening, at 20.30, Black section (F/Sgt J. Maier and Sgt Roovers) was ordered to patrol the Isle of Wight. Roovers was following his leader in a wide echelon right until Maier gave another vector. He looked around to see if Roovers had followed correctly, but there was no sign of him and he did not respond to calls over the R/T. Maier continued the patrol until relieved. He had hoped Roovers had returned to base following a R/T failure, but that was not the case. With darkness approaching, it was too late to launch an ASR mission. One was performed in the early hours of the 3rd, but nothing was found. The routine continued until the 19th when a *Ranger* was flown in conjunction with 91 Squadron (also equipped with Spitfire XIVs) and W/C Oxspring. Each unit provided three Spitfires. The CO, with Flying Officers L. Meijers and J. Jonker, participated in the raid. Two other pilots, Flying Officers van Arkel and Muller, had to abandon the op after having trouble with their 90 gallon auxiliary tanks (they later flew a reconnaissance over Boulogne where they spotted a large ship and duly reported its sighting on return). The Spitfires flew to Ostend, then flew to the south of Antwerp, turned north, flew over the aerodrome of Volkel, but the Germans based there did not react even though the Spitfires went over at 3000 feet, and came out via Rotterdam. The next day, 322 returned to its routine patrols, but was plagued by various incidents, fortunately with only minor consequences for aircraft and pilots, until the 31st when the second loss of the month occurred. In the early hours of the day, F/O J. Dekker and F/Sgt C. Kooy took off on a patrol, but Kooy found his aircraft nose heavy and difficult to fly as he had to hold the stick with both hands. He immediately called his leader and told him he was going to land. The weather conditions were such, however, that he could not see the ground so he asked control for a homing, but then found he could not steer the course as his arms were so tired that he had to use his legs as well. His speed at that time was 120 mph and his height 250 feet and, having tried without success to make base for about fifteen minutes, he decided to climb and bale out, informing control of his decision. He climbed with difficulty to 1800 feet and baled out successfully, his chute opening at 900 feet. He saw the Spitfire crash in flames 300 yards away. It was not a good day for the Dutch as F/Sgt G. Dijkman's right undercarriage collapsed, causing the aircraft to loop to the right with the wing touching the ground. He escaped injury and the Spitfire was later repaired. The bad weather during the first days of June limited the number of patrols flown. On 5 June, during the day, stripes were painted on the aircraft and late in the evening W/C Oxspring announced, in the presence of all pilots and the CO, that D-Day, the first day of the long anticipated invasion and the start of the liberation of Europe, had been fixed for the next day. The new codes 3W were also painted on the aircraft. The squadron's task was to fly high altitude patrols. Oxspring defined the limits of the assault area and gave a general idea of the initial phase, pointing at a map of the region involved that comprised the Cherbourg Peninsula up to the east of Le Havre. The squadron was asked to be ready by 04.30 the next morning. Dawn on the 6th saw everyone ready at 04.30, with some concern as the night had been windy and rainy, but by 07.30 the sky seemed to have cleared enough. As far as 322 was concerned, however, nothing happened before 15.15 when the squadron completed uneventful anti-reconnaissance patrols over the Isle of Wight. The following day was even worse, with only a section scramble to investigate an unidentified aircraft that turned out to be a Mosquito, but on the other hand, the weather was not as good as expected. While the number of patrols almost returned to normal on the 8th, they soon stopped as the weather steadily deteriorated. The bad weather also prevented any flying the next day. Patrols resumed in earnest on the 10th. The nature of the sorties changed a little on the 12th when 322 was tasked with escorting five Dakotas towing Waco gliders to Sainte-Mère-Église on the Cherbourg Peninsula. This was completed without incident. Further escorts for transport aircraft were carried out over the next few days. Most of the time, the task was completed without incident, but on the 16th F/Sgt F. van Valkenburg was hit by flak and had to make an emergency landing on a strip in Normandy (B4). Two days later 322 received an unexpected new assignment – anti-Diver patrols (intercepting V-1 flying bombs that had begun to hit the British Isles). The area assigned to 322 was between Halsham and Battle. This new tasking was received with great satisfaction as the pilots felt that at last they would be able to use their cannons for the first time since conversion to the Spitfire XIV. The first anti-Diver patrols were flown on 18 June at 13.15. It did not take long before the Dutch opened their score against the pilotless machines as Flying Officers R. Burgwal and L. Meijers shot down a V-1 each in the middle of the afternoon. Rudi Burgwal got his V-1 by firing at it from 600 yards (it exploded) while Meijers attacked from 400 yards and watched it turn over and hit the ground. Later, in the evening, another V-1 was shared by F/L L. van Eendenburg and F/O R. van Daalen Wetters. The following day, 322 added four more V-1s to its tally (two were shared with aircraft from other units, the first with a Tempest, the second with a Spitfire). Until the end of the month, anti-Diver patrols increased significantly with no less than 62 sorties flown on 29 June from West Malling, the new station the squadron had been operating from since the 20th. At the same time, the score of V-1s increased too with one claimed on the 20th, one on the 21st, three on the 22nd (F/L J. Plesman claimed the first of his eleven destroyed), two on the 23rd (including one for the CO), and seven (one shared) on the 27th. Flight Sergeant J. Harms got two, but a third was disallowed and eventually credited to a Tempest pilot. This rate of scoring continued with four more on the 28th (one shared), nine on the 29th, and five on the 30th. These were good results, but it was a dangerous game as, on the 29th, F/Sgt W. de Vries came close to being shot down by flak while attacking a V-1. His right aileron was blown out and he received holes in the right wing, engine cowling and fuselage, forcing him to land at Kingsnorth.

July started with the destruction of another V-1 by W/O J.A. Maier. The next day, 322 could not fly because of a low ceiling, causing some frustration as the V-1s continued to hit the country. It was not until the evening that flying resumed. The same scenario was

Major K.C. Kuhlmann SAAF, with a parrot in his hands, poses in the middle of the Dutch personnel of 322 Sqn. From left to right, F/L M. Muller, F/O C. Schudel (Medical Officer), F/O L. Wolters (†16.09.44), P/O Lockton (Intelligence Officer), Flying Officers R. Burgwall and J. Arts, F/L L. Eendenburg and F/O L.Meijers. Flying Officer Burgwall would later be posted missing over France on 12 August 1944 while F/O Wolters would be killed in an air collision soon after on 16 September.

Keith Cowie KUHLMANN
SAAF No. P102441

Joining the SAAF in July 1940, as a regular officer, Kuhlmann was posted to the UK early in 1942 on conclusion of his training in Southern Rhodesia. He was part of the first batch of fighter pilots who had volunteered for service with the RAF in the United Kingdom at the end of 1941. He served with No. 222 (Natal) Squadron but, in August 1942, he sailed for Malta where he was posted to No. 185 Squadron. A few days after his arrival he opened his score by shooting down a Ju88 on the 27th. Other claims followed over the coming weeks (he added three more aircraft destroyed, one probable and three damaged) until 19 October, the date of his last claim. When he left Malta, at the end of January 1943, he had become a Flight commander and a DFC was gazetted the following March.

After a period of rest at No. 57 OTU, he was posted at the end of August to No. 322 (Dutch) Squadron as Officer Commanding. Without making any further claims, he led the unit until 1 September 1944 when his
Spitfire Mk. IX was shot down by flak during an armed reconnaissance. He was taken prisoner and was released at the end of the war. He continued to serve in the SAAF after the war and retired as a Brigadier in 1973.

Supermarine Spitfire Mk.XIV NH718
No. 322 (Ducth) Squadron
Major K.C. Kuhlmann (SAAF)
West Malling (UK), June-July 1944

Spitfire XIV NH700/VL-P being washed in April 1944. In the foreground, participating in the task, is F/L van Eendenburg, one of the two flight commanders at the time and who would later, in September 1944, take over 322 Sqn after Major Kuhlmann was shot down and made a PoW. 'Kees' van Eendenburg survived the war. Before joining 322, he served with Nos. 41, 167, 118 Squadrons. He was among the first Dutch to succeed escaping to England, after the occupation of the Netherlands, as early as July 1940. This airframe was lost soon after on the 11th during an air test killing the pilot, F/O J.W. van Hamel.

repeated on 3 July, but 322 was able to fly patrols a bit earlier, in the middle of the afternoon, and in the evening three V-1s were destroyed. July 4 was a normal day of operations with continuous patrols from 04.35 to 23.35 hours. Flying Officers J. Jonker, R.F. Burgwal and F.W. Speetjens added a V-1 each, but Speetjens had a misadventure, when his engine cut two minutes after having destroyed the V-1, and he had to make a belly landing in a wheat field at Hever. He was not injured and the aircraft not seriously damaged. The next day, F/Sgt M. Janssen and F/L L. van Eendenburg claimed two V-1s each, but those were soon reduced to one and a half each, Janssen having to share his V-1 with a 1 Squadron Spitfire and van Eendenburg with a Polish pilot from 316 Squadron. Bad luck continued the next day when the claim made by F/Sgt H. Cram was disallowed. The Dutch got their revenge on the 7th when they claimed six V-1s destroyed, all being allowed. Among the victors was F/O Rudi Burgwal who had a narrow escape when his target exploded in mid-air after he had closed in from 200 yards to 100 yards. He made an emergency landing at Ashford. On the 8th 322 flew its first night sortie during which F/Sgt Cram destroyed a Diver at around 04.30 hours. During the day, seven more followed, including five for Burgwal alone! The next day Cram claimed two V-1s in three minutes. Flying continued after midnight and at 00.20 on the 10th F/L Plesman shot down a V-1. Flight Lieutenant van Eendenburg added another in the afternoon. The next day, five more were credited to five different Dutch pilots, followed by another five, and a sixth shared with a USAAF Mustang, the next day. The latter caused the death of a Dutchman, W/O J. Maier, when the flying bomb he was trying to tip with his wing was shot down by the Mustang. The Spitfire was caught in the explosion and it fell out of control and crashed. On the 13th, Flight Sergeants M. Janssen and J.. Harms got one Diver each, but unfortunately the weather stopped the hunt prematurely around

In June 1944, 322 Sqn switched squadron codes from 'VL' to '3W', using the latter until the end of war. This is Major Kuhlmann's mount, NH718/3W-G, in full D-Day markings. He, Jongbloed and Burgwal were successful against V-1s while flying in this aircraft. *(M. Schoeman)*

The top Dutch V-1 scorer was F/O Rudy Burgwal. Born in the Dutch East Indies, he escaped from Holland in September 1941 and joined the RAF on arrival. Trained, he was then posted to 322 Sqn in July 1943. He was posted missing, shortly after the conversion to Spitfire IXs, on 12 August while escorting Lancasters.

teatime. The weather remained fine on the 14th and four more V-1s were shot down by the Dutch, including two by F/L Plesman. The squadron scored two on the 16th, three on the 18th and another six on the 19th even though one had to be shared with another squadron. Plesman and F/O Burgwal, the top scorers of the squadron, were among the claimants. The next day, Plesman was patrolling Margate to Folkestone when he was told a Diver was coming in near Dover. He spotted it and attacked from 150 yards line astern. He saw strikes and the flying bomb crashed and exploded northeast of Ashford to make his eighth claim over a V-1. Less than an hour later, it was the turn of F/O M. van Bergen to score. On 22 July, the squadron moved to the advanced landing ground at Deanland, west of Hailsham, and, from the new base, 322 destroyed three more V-1s that day (including two for Burgwal). The next day Flying Officers G. Jongbloed and C. Manders added a Diver each to their tally. One was claimed on the 24th, shared by Burgwal and F/O J. Jonker, and another five (two being shared with other squadrons) followed on the 26th. Burgwal was once again in the mix. The squadron was now approaching the 100-kill mark and the question was who would claim it. On the 28th two V-1s were destroyed, one being credited to the South African CO, and two more were added to the tally on the 29th. A single victory on the 30th brought the score to 99. Everybody was expecting the 100th to be claimed the next day, but the weather prevented any flying! That's how July ended, a month that saw the completion of no less than 1026 sorties.

The day everyone was waiting for came on 2 August. The previous bad weather also prevented any flying before 17.00 hours, but no Diver was seen. The achievement of the century was made in a strange manner as the two claims made by F/Sgt R. van Beers at 12.54 and 13.00 respectively near the Tunbridge Wells area had to be shared, the first with a 3 Squadron Tempest and the second with the pilot of a 91 Squadron Spitfire XIV. The two half claims could not count for a full claim so negotiations were opened with 91 Squadron with a view to asking them to give up the half share. Flight Lieutenant R.S. Nash, of 91 Squadron, generously withdrew his half claim making van Beers the pilot who claimed the 100th flying bomb for the Dutch. The squadron had to wait until the 4th to score again, Flight Lieutenants J. van Arkel and J. Plesman shooting down one V-1 each. The day before, 322 had received some ten new Spitfire XIVs armed with two 0.50-in machine guns instead of the outdated four 0.303-in armament. Further aircraft followed over the next few days. The squadron's scoreboard was increased by three more V-1s on 5 August (two for F/O R. Burgwal's account), one on 6 August, another on the night of 7 August, and a single night kill late on the 8th. The same day 322 was notified it would exchange the Spitfire XIVs for Spitfire IXs in order to carry out another task. This could have been the last of the V-1 claims, but while the squadron was released from dawn on the 9th until 12.30 on the 10th, F/L Plesman made three anti-Diver patrols that night, the first between 22.30 and 24.00, the second from 01.00 to 02.50, and the last one between 04.30 and 05.30. Eight minutes after taking off for his third night patrol, Plesman was warned a Diver was approaching and he was vectored to the interception. He attacked line astern from a range of 200 yards. He saw strikes and it exploded on the ground in an open field. This was the last V-1 destroyed by the Dutch. More than 250 sorties were flown by the Spitfire XIVs in August out of 2580 flown in all on type.

After having participated in the V-1 hunt with its Spitfire XIVs, 322 Squadron was tasked with a new role in August 1944 and returned to the Ramrods (escorts) it had flown while flying the Spitfire Mk.V. It was with much regret that the exchange of aircraft took place at Hawkinge on 9 August. Unfortunately, in returning to 322's base, Deanland, Flying Officer A. Homburg crashed on landing; his Spitfire caught fire, but he managed to get out safely despite receiving first degree burns to his hand that required treatment at hospital. This was far from a good start for the unit's association with the Mk.IX, but what would follow would be even more dramatic! The next two days were spent preparing the machines for the next escort which eventually took place on the 11th. The Dutch were still working with No. 91 Squadron which had also just traded its Spitfire XIVs for IXs. The first escort was, as mentioned, carried out on the 11th, covering 120 Lancasters targeting marshalling yards at Douai (*Ramrod* 1186), the two squadrons taking care of the rear half of the bomber formation. The wing leader, W/C R.X. Oxspring, flew with 322 on this occasion. Later that day, ten Halifaxes heading to bomb a Noball target (V-weapon sites) in France were also escorted (*Ramrod* 1188). Both ops were uneventful. The next day, however, a tragic event occurred. On another escort (*Ramrod* 1190), F/O J. Jonker developed engine trouble and was obliged to turn for home, escorted by F/O R. Burgwal. He landed safely at Rennes aerodrome (the fate of the Spitfire remains unclear) but lost touch with Burgwal who was reported missing. He was the top V-1 scorer of the squadron, and

Leendert Carel Marie van Eendenburg
RAF No. 108814

'Kees' van Eendenburg was born in the NEI. When war broke out, he was still a student in the Netherlands, while serving as a reserve artillery officer in the Dutch Army. In May 1940, the Netherlands were occupied and out of the war in five days. He managed to escape to England in July 1940. First enlisting in the Royal Navy in August 1940, he was transferred to the RAF in February 1941. He completed his training and, in December 1941, was posted to No. 41 Squadron. He made his first claim, an Fw190 destroyed, on 3 May 1942 but was posted to No. 167 (Gold Coast) Squadron in July. This unit had one of its two flights manned by Dutch aircrew. He remained with 167 until May 1943 during which he added one shared confirmed victory. In June 1943, the flight was raised to full squadron strength and became No. 322 (Dutch) Squadron. He became one of its flight commanders in February 1944, a position he held until being promoted OC in September. During that time he destroyed seven V-1s in flight. He led the squadron until November. He was then posted to HQFC but continued to fly operationally from time to time. He was transferred to the new RNethAF in February 1946 and retired two years later.

Supermarine Spitfire Mk IX MK265
No. 322 (Dutch) Squadron
Squadron Leader L. van Eendenburg
Hawkinge (UK), September 1944

Kees van Eenderburg showing his Spitfire Mk IX to Princess Juliana. (*Netherlands Institute for Military History, The Hague*)

therefore top Dutch scorer, with nineteen claimed destroyed. Escorts continued until the end of the month, the squadron flying almost every day, sometimes three times a day. From the 23rd onwards, some Rodeos were carried out alongside the regular escorts and several armed recces. This gave the Dutch the chance to attack some targets of opportunity. These were more dangerous than simple escorts, however, and while strafing some METs during an armed recce in the Calais-Aulnoye-Ghent area, F/Sgt R. van Beers developed engine trouble, possibly hit by ground fire, and turned for home. His engine soon failed, so he told F/Sgt J. Harms, who had accompanied him, he would bale out over the Channel. A few days later, on the 30th, and in the same area, it was the turn of F/O M. Muller to be hit by flak. He was heard to say he was baling out and was eventually posted missing. Fortunately, he managed to evade capture and was back with the squadron on 11 September. The last day of August consisted of one Ramrod (No 1250) and an armed recce, both uneventful, for a total of 320 sorties for the month, but at a cost of four Spitfires and two pilots lost. Even during the Spitfire XIV era, 322 had not known such losses. Worse was yet to come. On 1 September the squadron took off at 07.12 for an armed reconnaissance over the usual Calais-Ghent-Aulnoye area; four METs and one light AFV were destroyed. Another MET and AFV were also damaged. While going down to shoot up something he had seen, the CO, Major Kuhlmann, was apparently hit by flak and had to bale out about five miles inland near Cap Griz-Nez. His number two saw him land and wave. He was captured soon after. The squadron returned without its CO and took off again at 10.27 for another armed reconnaissance in the same area; this time a gun post was attacked and two METs damaged. The flak was very accurate once more; this time F/L L. van Eendenburg, the A Flight CO, was hit and made a forced landing south-east of Lille, while F/L J. Plesman, the B Flight CO, had his tail shot off. He was seen to spin in north-east of Saint-Omer. He was not seen leaving his aircraft and was indeed killed in the subsequent crash. Kees van Eendenburg's luck held and he managed to evade capture to return to England eleven days later. In a single day, the squadron had lost its CO and two flight commanders, a severe blow for the Dutch who were already suffering a shortage of leaders and pilots for their flying units. Severe gales over the next few days prevented operational flying. This gave the squadron time to recover from the loss of its leaders and appoint replacements. As an immediate measure, command was given to F/L W. de Wolff (the new A Flight CO), but soon after temporary command was transferred to F/L J. van Arkel (the new B Flight CO) who held the position until a new CO was appointed. When, on 12 September, F/L van Eendenburg returned to 322 after his escape, he assumed command. In the meantime, operations resumed and it soon became obvious the period of bad luck had yet to run its course. On 16 September, the squadron was called to participate in a late afternoon armed recce over the The Hague-Den Helder-Amsterdam-Utrecht. Shortly after take-off Flying Officers C. Manders and D. Wolters collided while climbing through cloud in line astern. Wolters crashed near Hawkinge and was killed while Manders baled out and landed safely. Despite this, the squadron continued its armed recce and escort work and soon had its first encounter with the Luftwaffe while escorting glider-towing Dakotas over Holland during Operation Market. Patrolling the Eindhoven area, Flying Officers P. Cramerus and G. Jongbloed spotted enemy aircraft attacking a returning Dakota. Cramerus reported to the wing leader (W/C Oxspring) who ordered the formation to drop its auxiliary fuel tanks. An attack followed at once. Cramerus engaged the Fw190 attacking the Dakota, closed in and fired a short burst of cannon and machine guns from about 200 yards; no results were observed. The Fw190 rolled on its back at which time Cramerus got him in his sight again. He fired another, longer, burst of two seconds and saw strikes on the wing roots and fuselage. The Fw190 dived and was last seen entering cloud at 4000 feet in a vertical dive. It was claimed as damaged while F/O Jongbloed claimed another Fw190 as damaged. The Dutch went back over the bridges as cover for Operation *Market* and then returned to its conventional escort duties, but the rest of the month proved uneventful. At the beginning of October, the pilots were advised they were going to attend a course on bombing, and air-to-ground and air-to-air firing, meaning the squadron's role would change to close

Wearing the Dutch orange triangle under the cockpit, Spitfire Mk.IX MJ360/3W-K receives some final attention from the groundcrew before its next flight. Note the Spitfire's underside which was prone to weathering and staining from oil leaks, mud and dust. The invasion stripes, which were often hastily and crudely applied, had a rough surface on which such weathering appeared much faster than on the parts of the fuselage where the factory-applied, spray-painted paint coat was much smoother. This explains that on many photos the invasion stripes appear completely black on the parts of the fuselage most exposed to weathering.

air support. The course was scheduled to be held at Fairwood Common from the 10th. Therefore, the squadron was stood down, but a last op, *Ramrod* 1319, an escort for Halifaxes bombing Cleves, was carried out on the 7th. In the middle of the course, personnel were notified that, as the course was completed, the squadron would re-equip with Spitfire XVIs (more suitable for the new tasks to be carried out). At the end of October, 322 moved to Biggin Hill and, on the 4th, an exchange of machines was made, the pilots trading their Spitfire IXs for brand new XVIs at 84 GSU. This exchange ended a somewhat painful association between the Dutch and the Spitfire IX.

When the last Mk.IX sortie was carried out, the squadron was based in England at Deanland under the command of S/L L. van Eendenburg, a Dutchman. Over the days that followed, questions were raised about the future of 322 and, during the month, it was accepted the unit would be deployed to the Continent with Spitfire Mk.XVIs. In any case, changes would have to wait until after the completion of the APC at Fairwood Common, which took place between 10 and 30 October. The next day, 322 flew to Biggin Hill and, over the next few days, flew its 19 Mk.IXs to 84 GSU, returning with the same number of Mk.XVIs on the 4th. All the pilots seemed quite pleased with the performance of their new mount. Preparation for the move began the next day, without S/L Eendenburg as he relinquished command on the 17th to S/L H.F. O'Neill, a pilot who had so far served most of his war in the Mediterranean. During the month, pilots practiced fighter-bomber tactics, the new role assigned to 322. By December, the

Groundcrew preparing a Spitfire XVI for the next op during Winter 1944–45. Bombs are already installed under the wings.

Spitfire RK893/3W-A during Winter 1944–45, bombs ready. It was lost on 13 February 1945 with its pilot.

squadron was ready to fly to the Continent, but bad weather and other administrative issues postponed the departure until the last day of the month. The destination was B.79/Woensdrecht under No. 132 (Norwegian) Wing's authority. Operations started on 4 January; the squadron contributed 11 aircraft to a fighter sweep in the Rheine area. No enemy aircraft were seen but 322 claimed one eastbound loco as damaged. A second show, a dive-bombing attack on crossroads just north of the River Maas, was flown later with five aircraft. The Dutch tried to get airborne as soon as the weather permitted but, in January 1945, many days were not flyable. Despite this, about 185 sorties were carried out for the month at a cost of one pilot, F/Sgt C. Kooij, who was seen crashing during an attack on a so-called 'saboteur school' in the Doorn area on the 28th. It is believed he was caught in the bomb blast from the preceding aircraft. In February, 322 was engaged more often and managed to perform just over 300 sorties, coupled with a move to Schijndel on the 22nd. But the cost was high. On 13 February, F/O E. Ditmarsch was shot down and killed during the first show of day attacking motorised transport (MET) near Geldern. In the afternoon, it was the turn of F/Sgt A.J. Bary to be shot down in the same area; experiencing a glycol leak, probably caused by flak, he was wounded but managed to survive as a PoW. Just before midday the following day, another armed recce was carried out and METs attacked near Straelen. Flying Officer Frans J.H. van Eijk was hit in the tail and caught fire. He tried to make a safe landing but failed; the Spitfire spun into the ground and, while van Eijk was seen to bale out, he did not survive. The last three losses took place on the 24th and 25th, all writing off the aircraft involved. On the 24th, F/L R. van Daalen Wetters returned to base with wrinkled mainplanes, after pulling out hard from a dive, and, the next day, another armed recce claimed two Spitfires badly damaged. Both pilots, F/O P. Cramerus and Sgt L. Knappert, managed to return to base, but the Spitfires were only good for scrap. Sadly, alongside these operational losses, 322 had to add F/O J. Koes who was killed on the 3rd during a training flight when his Spitfire was seen to break up in flight. March, if we ignore a change of command on the 2nd (S/L Bram van der Stok taking over, S/L O'Neill becoming Wing Leader 132 Wing), was almost identical to February with 335 sorties flown and the same number of aircraft lost. On 5 March, after ten minutes of an armed recce, F/O J. Vlug called up to say he had seen some METs on a road near Xanten and was going down to investigate/attack. Later, he was heard say-

The war is over. Some Dutch pilots are gathered chatting near a Spitfire (possible TD369) at Wunsdorf. Left to right: W/O J. Bakker (previously with No. 132 Squadron), P/O M. Janssen (former NEI), W/O J. van Rosendaal (previously served with No. 222 Squadron), and F/O R. Groeneveld (former NEI). (*Netherlands Institute for Military History, The Hague*)

Spitfire TD369/3W-H being warmed up before the next flight during the summer of 1945 (no bombs carried). It was issued to 322 early in April 1945.
(*Netherlands Institute for Military History, The Hague*)

ing he wanted to go home straightaway, possibly after being hit by ground fire. Soon after, he was heard again, saying he was just north of Wesel and was not going to make it. He died in the subsequent crash and was found in the cockpit. Two weeks later, 322 was hit by misfortune when F/Sgt S.D. Lazarus was killed in a practice flight after the Spitfire he was flying exploded without reason. On 26 March, various armed recces were carried out in the afternoon. Heading to the Zwolle–Eschele–Emmerich area, the patrol led by F/L W. de Wolff found a target of opportunity and strafed a horse-drawn transport; no results were observed. However, moderate flak was noticed which probably hit the Spitfire flown by Sgt T.M. Biallosterski; soon the engine developed trouble, leading the pilot to make a forced landing. The aircraft caught fire on landing, but Biallosterski was rescued with light burns and bruises by two civilians. He was of Dutch origin but had been recruited in Canada where he had been living for years. The last loss of the month took place on the 30th when 322 took part in a level bombing attack on the German HQ at Zutphen. Hits were obtained on both houses in the target area and intense flak was experienced, hitting two Spitfires. Flight Sergeant Jess was obliged to a make a forced landing not far from base, without major consequences for him; the Spitfire was eventually written off in April. Warrant Officer H. Cramm, however, was shot down and killed near the target.

In April, despite those severe losses, 322 managed to provide support to Allied troops, putting more pressure on the collapsing German forces; 400 sorties were achieved. That rate of effort was accompanied by two moves, B106/Twente on the 18th and B.113/Varrelbusch on the 30th. However, April started badly, the squadron losing four Spitfires to flak in the Zutphen area during the only operation of the day, an armed recce in the Deventer–Zwolle–Meppen–Lingen–Hengelo area. Pilot Officer M. Janssen survived and was later found in a Canadian hospital. Flying Officer J. van Roosendaal was taken prisoner but soon managed to escape. Flying Officer L. Hendriks crashed near Warken and was injured while F/O A. Homberg was killed. Two weeks later, attacking METs in the Emden–Leer area, flak hit the aircraft flown by F/Sgt G. Dijkman who was obliged to make a forced landing in the Allied lines. He was safe, but the Spitfire was written off due to the end of the war being within sight. The next day, while on an armed recce in central Holland, F/Sgt M. Rackwitz developed an engine failure and was obliged to make a forced landing in enemy held territory and spent the last days of the war in Europe as a PoW. He was another pilot with an interesting heritage, being of Dutch origin but joining up while living in Argentina. A few days later, on the 23rd, F/O K. Norman, a British pilot, also developed

'Bob' van der Stok was Dutch but from the Netherlands East Indies. He joined the Dutch Air Force in 1936 and when war hit the Netherlands, he was a fighter pilot flying the Fokker D.XXI. On the first day of the invasion, he managed to destroy a Bf109 and damage another. Sent back to civilian life, he formed a resistance cell and made three unsuccessful attempts to reach Great Britain. He finally succeeded and arrived in September 1941. Having been trained as a fighter pilot, his re-training was short and in February 1941 he was posted to No. 41 Squadron. In March and April 1942, he added a confirmed Bf109 and three damaged aircraft to his credit but his scoring was cut short on the 12th when he was shot down and became a PoW. In the following years he tried to escape many times and was eventually successful during the 'Great Escape' from Sagan in March 1944. While many of the escapers were later recaptured, and some executed, van der Stok was one of the three who were able to return to the UK. He finally made the 'home run' in July 1944. Following a refresher course, he was initially posted to No. 74 (Trinidad) Squadron, in mid-February 1945 and was given command of No. 322 (Dutch) Squadron early in March 1945 and led this unit until the end of the war. In that time, he completed about 20 sorties without adding to his tally. He left 322 in October that year. After the war he emigrated to the USA.

Supermarine Spitfire Mk.XVI TD137
No. 322 (Ducth) Squadron
Squadron Leader B. van der Stok
B.116/Wünsdorf (Germany), summer 1945

engine trouble, just after making an attack near Linden, and made a forced landing while F/Sgt S. Aertsen, flying with another section on the same op, saw his engine cut in the circuit at Twente; he overshot his landing and overturned. He was safe but the Spitfire wrecked. The last week of the European war was intense with over 100 sorties carried out, a high rate considering there was no flying on the 29th and the 30th, but no major incident was recorded. In May, 22 ops were flown on the 3rd and the 4th during which the guns were used for the last time against trains and trucks found on morning sorties. Three days later, on the 7th, S/L van der Stok led 322 on a patrol of Bremen, which was carried out without incident. On landing at 10.15, 322 Squadron's war was over. The next day, a flypast took place, but it ended badly for 322. Flight Lieutenant D.J. Hunter's aircraft developed engine trouble and he tried to make a forced landing on the airfield; in trying to avoid a lorry in his path, having no engine power at all, his Spitfire hit the ground and disintegrated. He was severely injured and sadly succumbed later in the evening. He was an American from Arizona serving in the RAF. The squadron moved to B.116/Wunsdorf on 2 July where it remained until disbanded on 7 October. During this time, 322 recorded a Spitfire wrecked following an engine failure on the 24th during a practice formation. The pilot, F/Sgt T.M. Biallosterski, escaped injury but the Spitfire would not fly again.

Above:
Spitfire 3W-J being serviced at open space during the summer of 1945.
(CT Collection)

Left:
Spitfire TE247/3W-V at the end of the war. It had a teardrop canopy and was received by the squadron during the first days of April 1945.

A formation of three Spitfire XVIs over Germany during the summer of 1945; the CO, S/L van der Stok, is leading.

Date	Pilot	SN	Origin	Type	Serial	Code	Nb	Cat.
18.06.44	F/O Rudolph **Burgwal**	RAF No. 113893	(NL)/RAF	V-1		3W-K	1.0	C
	F/O Lourens **Meijers**	RAF No. 136569	(NL)/RAF	V-1	**NH686**	3W-M	1.0	C
	F/L Leendert van **Eendenburg**	RAF No. 108814	(NL)/RAF	V-1	**RB184**	3W-B	0.5	C
	F/O Rudolf van **Daalen Wetters**	RAF No. 104590	(NL)/RAF			3W-K	0.5	C
19.06.44	F/O Rudolph **Burgwal**	RAF No. 113893	(NL)/RAF	V-1		3W-D	0.5	C
	F/O Pieter **Cramerus**	RAF No. 143220	(NL)/RAF	V-1		3W-N	1.0	C
	F/O Jan **Dekker**	RAF No. 135761	(NL)/RAF	V-1		3W-U	1.0	C
	F/O Gerard **Jongbloed**	RAF No. 104592	(NL)/RAF	V-1	**RB184**	3W-B	0.5	C
20.06.44	F/L Leendert van **Eendenburg**	RAF No. 108814	(NL)/RAF	V-1	**RB184**	3W-B	1.0	C
21.06.44	F/Sgt Ronald van **Beers**	RAF No. 1814965	(NL)/RAF	V-1		3W-K	1.0	C
22.06.44	F/L Jan **Plesman**	RAF No. 102524	(NL)/RAF	V-1		3W-V	1.0	C
	F/O Coenraad **Manders**	RAF No. 113889	(NL)/RAF	V-1		3W-U	1.0	C
	F/O Rudolf van **Daalen Wetters**	RAF No.104590	(NL)/RAF	V-1		3W-J	1.0	C
23.06.44	F/O Jan van **Arkel**	RAF No. 124639	(NL)/RAF	V-1		3W-V	0.50	C
	F/O Mijnard L. van **Bergen**	RAF No. 113896	(NL)/RAF			3W-N	0.50	C
	Maj Keith C. **Kuhlmann**	SAAF No. P102441	SAAF	V-1	**NH718**	3W-G	1.0	C
27.06.44	F/Sgt Ronald L. van **Beers**	RAF No. 1814965	(NL)/RAF	V-1		3W-H	1.0	C
	F/Sgt Cornelis **Kooy**	RAF No. 1814967	(NL)/RAF	V-1	**RM678**	3W-Q	0.50	C
	F/Sgt Johannes **Harms**	RAF No. 1814945	(NL)/RAF	V-1		3W-J	2.0	C
	F/L Jan **Plesman**	RAF No. 102524	(NL)/RAF	V-1		3W-V	1.0	C
	F/O Mijnard van **Bergen**	RAF No. 113896	(NL)/RAF	V-1		3W-N	1.0	C
	F/O Jan van **Arkel**	RAF No. 124639	(NL)/RAF	V-1		3W-T	1.0	C
28.06.44	F/O Lambert **Wolters**	RAF No. 141896	(NL)/RAF	V-1		3W-N	0.50	C
	W/O Justin **Maier**	RAF No. 1549995	(NL)/RAF	V-1	**RM678**	3W-Q	1.0	C
	F/O Gerard **Jongbloed**	RAF No. 104592	(NL)/RAF	V-1		3W-C	1.0	C
	F/Sgt Frederik van **Valkenburg**	RAF No. 1814944	(NL)/RAF	V-1	**NH649**	3W-F	1.0	C
29.06.44	F/O Frans **Speetjens**	RAF No. 145140	(NL)/RAF	V-1		3W-J	1.0	C
	F/O Gerard **Jongbloed**	RAF No. 104592	(NL)/RAF	V-1		3W-K	1.0	C
	F/Sgt Martin **Janssen**	RAF No. 1814942	(NL)/RAF	V-1		3W-D	1.0	C
	F/O Rudolph **Burgwall**	RAF No. 113893	(NL)/RAF	V-1	**NH649**	3W-F	2.0	C
	F/O Martin **Muller**	RAF No. 135760	(NL)/RAF	V-1		3W-T	1.0	C
	F/L Jan **Plesman**	RAF No. 102524	(NL)/RAF	V-1		3W-W	1.0	C
	F/O Lambert **Wolters**	RAF No. 141896	(NL)/RAF	V-1		3W-N	1.0	C
	F/O Frans van **Eijk**	RAF No.113894	(NL)/RAF	V-1	**NH699**	3W-R	1.0	C
	F/Sgt Willem de **Vries**	RAF No. 1814947	(NL)/RAF	V-1	**RM678**	3W-Q	1.0	C
30.06.44	F/O Lourens **Meijers**	RAF No. 136569	(NL)/RAF	V-1		3W-J	1.0	C
	F/O Jan van **Arkel**	RAF No. 124639	(NL)/RAF	V-1		3W-D	1.0	C
	F/O Rudolph **Burgwal**	RAF No. 113893	(NL)/RAF	V-1	**RB171**	3W-E	2.0	C
	F/O Jan **Jonker**	RAF No. 132082	(NL)/RAF	V-1		3W-K	1.0	C
01.07.44	W/O Justin **Maier**	RAF No. 1549995	(NL)/RAF	V-1		3W-T	1.0	C
03.07.44	F/Sgt Frederik **Cramm**	RAF No. 1692491	(NL)/RAF	V-1	**NH699**	3W-R	1.0	C
	F/O Jan **Jonker**	RAF No. 132082	(NL)/RAF	V-1	**RB160**	3W-A	1.0	C
	F/O Frans van **Eijk**	RAF No.113894	(NL)/RAF	V-1		3W-U	0.5	C
	P/O Aart **Homburg**	RAF No.125169	(NL)/RAF			3W-Y	0.5	C
04.07.44	F/O Jan **Jonker**	RAF No. 132082	(NL)/RAF	V-1		3W-D	1.0	C
	F/O Rudolph **Burgwal**	RAF No. 113893	(NL)/RAF	V-1	**NH649**	3W-F	1.0	C
	F/O Frans **Speetjens**	RAF No. 145140	(NL)/RAF	V-1	**RB160**	3W-A	1.0	C
05.07.44	F/Sgt Martin **Janssen**	RAF No. 1814942	(NL)/RAF	V-1		3W-D	1.5	C
	F/L Leendert van **Eendenburg**	RAF No. 108814	(NL)/RAF	V-1	**RB184**	3W-B	1.5	C
07.07.44	F/O Rudolph **Burgwall**	RAF No. 113893	(NL)/RAF	V-1		3W-C	1.0	C
	F/Sgt Cornelis **Kooy**	RAF No. 1814967	(NL)/RAF	V-1		3W-N	1.0	C

Two Dutch V-1 aces:
Left, Gerald F.J. Jongbloed served with 131 Sqn before joining 322. He later flew Tempests with 222 Sqn where he made his last V-1 claim. He survived the war. *(A.Thomas)*
Below, Jan van Arkel reached England as early as May 1940. After a short spell as a driver for the Dutch defence minister in London, he enlisted in the RAF in March 1941. After his training was completed, he was posted to 41 Sqn and then joined the Dutch flight of 167 Sqn, which became 322 Sqn in June 1943. He survived the war and continued his military career in the new RNethAF until 1974.
(Collections Nederlands Instituut voor Militaire Historie - NIMH)

Date	Name	No.	Service	Type	Serial	Code	Score	
	F/Sgt Gerard **Dijkman**	RAF No. 1814946	(NL)/RAF	*V-1*		3W-Y	1.0	C
	F/O Martin **Muller**	RAF No. 135760	(NL)/RAF	*V-1*		3W-W	1.0	C
	W/O Justin **Maier**	RAF No. 1549995	(NL)/RAF	*V-1*	**NH686**	3W-M	1.0	C
	F/O Pieter **Cramerus**	RAF No. 143220	(NL)/RAF	*V-1*		3W-V	1.0	C
08.07.44	F/Sgt Frederik **Cramm**	RAF No. 1692491	(NL)/RAF	*V-1*		3W-T	1.0	C
	F/O Rudolph **Burgwal**	RAF No. 113893	(NL)/RAF	*V-1*	**NH718**	3W-G	4.5	C
	F/O Jan **Jonker**	RAF No. 132082	(NL)/RAF	*V-1*		3W-K	1.0	C
	F/L Leendert **van Eendenburg**	RAF No. 108814	(NL)/RAF	*V-1*	**RB184**	3W-B	1.0	C
09.07.44	F/Sgt Frederik **Cramm**	RAF No. 1692491	(NL)/RAF	*V-1*	**NH699**	3W-R	2.0	C
10.07.44	F/L Jan **Plesman**	RAF No. 102524	(NL)/RAF	*V-1*		3W-W	1.0	C
	F/L Leendert **van Eendenburg**	RAF No. 108814	(NL)/RAF	*V-1*	**RB184**	3W-B	1.0	C
11.07.44	F/O Lourens **Meijers**	RAF No. 136569	(NL)/RAF	*V-1*		3W-H	1.0	C
	F/O Martin **Muller**	RAF No. 135760	(NL)/RAF	*V-1*		3W-T	1.0	C
	F/O Coenraad **Manders**	RAF No. 113889	(NL)/RAF	*V-1*		3W-V	1.0	C
	F/O Frans **van Eijk**	RAF No.113894	(NL)/RAF	*V-1*		3W-U	1.0	C
	W/O Justin **Maier**	RAF No. 1549995	(NL)/RAF	*V-1*	**NH686**	3W-M	1.0	C
12.07.44	F/O Coenraad **Manders**	RAF No. 113889	(NL)/RAF	*V-1*		3W-V	1.0	C
	F/Sgt Martin **Janssen**	RAF No. 1814942	(NL)/RAF	*V-1*	**RB171**	3W-E	2.0	C
	F/O Johannes **Vlug**	RAF No. 145141	(NL)/RAF	*V-1*	**RB160**	3W-A	1.0	C
	F/O Gerard **Jongbloed**	RAF No. 104592	(NL)/RAF	*V-1*	**NH718**	3W-G	1.0	C
	W/O Justin **Maier**	RAF No. 1549995	(NL)/RAF	*V-1*	**RM678**	3W-Q	0.5	C
13.07.44	F/Sgt Martin **Janssen**	RAF No. 1814942	(NL)/RAF	*V-1*	**RB160**	3W-A	1.0	C
	F/Sgt Johannes **Harms**	RAF No. 1814945	(NL)/RAF	*V-1*	**RB141**	3W-L	1.0	C
14.07.44	F/Sgt Ronald **van Beers**	RAF No. 1814965	(NL)/RAF	V-1		3W-H	1.0	C
	F/Sgt Martin **Janssen**	RAF No. 1814942	(NL)/RAF	V-1		3W-C	1.0	C
	F/L Jan **Plesman**	RAF No. 102524	(NL)/RAF	V-1		3W-W	2.0	C
16.07.44	F/O Gerard **Jongbloed**	RAF No. 104592	(NL)/RAF	V-1	**NH718**	3W-G	1.0	C
	F/O Jan **van Arkel**	RAF No. 124639	(NL)/RAF	V-1		3W-V	1.0	C
18.07.44	F/L Leendert **van Eendenburg**	RAF No. 108814	(NL)/RAF	V-1	**RB160**	3W-A	1.0	C
	F/O Johannes **Vlug**	RAF No. 145141	(NL)/RAF	V-1		3W-K	2.0	C
19.07.44	F/L Leendert **van Eendenburg**	RAF No. 108814	(NL)/RAF	V-1	**RB184**	3W-B	1.0	C
	F/O Gerard **Jongbloed**	RAF No. 104592	(NL)/RAF	V-1	**RB171**	3W-E	0.5	C
	F/O Johannes **Vlug**	RAF No. 145141	(NL)/RAF			3W-D	0.5	C
	F/O Rudolph **Burgwal**	RAF No. 113893	(NL)/RAF	V-1	**NH649**	3W-F	1.0	C
	F/L Jan **Plesman**	RAF No. 102524	(NL)/RAF	V-1		3W-W	1.0	C
	F/O Gerard **Jongbloed**	RAF No. 104592	(NL)/RAF	V-1	**RB171**	3W-E	1.0	C
	F/O Pieter **Cramerus**	RAF No. 143220	(NL)/RAF	V-1		3W-U	0.5	C
20.07.44	F/L Jan **Plesman**	RAF No. 102524	(NL)/RAF	V-1		3W-W	1.0	C
	F/O Mijnard **van Bergen**	RAF No. 113896	(NL)/RAF	V-1		3W-U	1.0	C
22.07.44	F/O Gerard **Jongbloed**	RAF No. 104592	(NL)/RAF	V-1	**RB171**	3W-E	1.0	C
	F/O Rudolph **Burgwal**	RAF No. 113893	(NL)/RAF	V-1		3W-C	2.0	C
23.07.44	F/O Gerard **Jongbloed**	RAF No. 104592	(NL)/RAF	V-1	**RB171**	3W-E	1.0	C
	F/O Coenraad **Manders**	RAF No. 113889	(NL)/RAF	V-1		3W-Y	1.0	C
24.07.44	F/O Rudolph **Burgwal**	RAF No. 113893	(NL)/RAF	V-1		3W-K	0.5	C
	F/O Jan **Jonker**	RAF No. 132082	(NL)/RAF			3W-D	0.5	C
26.07.44	F/O Jan **van Arkel**	RAF No. 124639	(NL)/RAF	V-1		3W-W	1.0	C
	F/Sgt Cornelis **Kooy**	RAF No. 1814967	(NL)/RAF	V-1		3W-S	1.0	C
	F/O Rudolph **Burgwal**	RAF No. 113893	(NL)/RAF	V-1	**NH649**	3W-F	1.0	C
	F/O Rudolph **Burgwal**	RAF No. 113893	(NL)/RAF	V-1	**NH649**	3W-F	0.5	C
	F/O Rudolph **Burgwal**	RAF No. 113893	(NL)/RAF	V-1	**NH649**	3W-F	0.5	C
28.07.44	F/Sgt Martin **Janssen**	RAF No. 1814942	(NL)/RAF	V-1		3W-D	0.5	C
	Maj Keith C. **Kuhlmann**	SAAF No. P102441	SAAF	V-1	**NH718**	3W-G	1.0	C
29.07.44	F/O Mijnard **van Bergen**	RAF No. 113896	(NL)/RAF	V-1		3W-T	1.0	C
	F/O Lambert **Wolters**	RAF No. 141896	(NL)/RAF	V-1		3W-N	0.5	C
30.07.44	F/O Rudolph **Burgwal**	RAF No. 113893	(NL)/RAF	V-1		3W-C	1.0	C
02.08.44	F/Sgt Ronald **van Beers**	RAF No. 1814965	(NL)/RAF	V-1		3W-C	0.5	C
	F/Sgt Ronald **van Beers**	RAF No. 1814965	(NL)/RAF	V-1		3W-C	1.0	C
04.08.44	F/O Jan **van Arkel**	RAF No. 124639	(NL)/RAF	V-1		3W-W	1.0	C

	F/L Jan **PLESMAN**	RAF No. 102524	(NL)/RAF	*V-1*		3W-Z	1.0	C
05.08.44	F/O Jan **JONKER**	RAF No. 132082	(NL)/RAF	*V-1*		3W-K	1.0	C
	F/O Rudolph **BURGWAL**	RAF No. 113893	(NL)/RAF	*V-1*	**RB184**	3W-B	2.0	C
06.08.44	F/L Jan **PLESMAN**	RAF No. 102524	(NL)/RAF	*V-1*		3W-P	1.0	C
07.08.44	F/O Rudolph **BURGWAL**	RAF No. 113893	(NL)/RAF	*V-1*		3W-L	1.0	C
09.08.44	F/L Leendert **VAN EENDENBURG**	RAF No. 108814	(NL)/RAF	*V-1*		3W-I	1.0	C
10.08.44	F/L Jan **PLESMAN**	RAF No. 102524	(NL)/RAF	*V-1*		3W-W	1.0	C

Total: 119.0 V-1s

Summary of the aircraft lost on Operations - 322 Squadron

Date	Pilot	S/N	Origin	Serial	Code	Fate
			SPITFIRE Mk V			
28.01.44	F/O Egbert **VAN NAGELL**	RAF No. 132084	(NL)/RAF	**AB818**	VL-N	†
			SPITFIRE Mk XIV			
02.05.44	Sgt Henric **ROOVERS**	RAF No. 1814943	(NL)/RAF	**RB141**	VL-L	†
31.05.44	F/Sgt Cornelis **KOOY**	RAF No. 1814967	(NL)/RAF	**NH687**	VL-Q	-
12.07.44	W/O Justin **MAIER**	RAF No. 1549995	(NL)/RAF	**RM678**	3W-Q	†
			SPITFIRE Mk IX			
12.08.44	F/O Rudolph **BURGWAL**	RAF No. 113893	(NL)/RAF	**MH370**	3W-L	†
26.08.44	F/Sgt Ronald **VAN BEERS**	RAF No. 1814965	(NL)/RAF	**MJ232**	3W-C	PoW
30.08.44	F/O Martin **MULLER**	RAF No. 135760	(NL)/RAF	**MK684**	3W-V	Eva.
01.09.44	Maj Keith C. **KUHLMANN**	SAAF No. P102441	SAAF	**MK905**	3W-G	PoW
	F/L Leendert **VAN EENDENBURG**	RAF No. 108814	(NL)/RAF	**PL238**	3W-E	Eva.
	F/L Jan **PLESMAN**	RAF No. 102524	(NL)/RAF	**MJ343**	3W-P	†
16.09.44	F/O Lambert **WOLTERS**	RAF No. 141896	(NL)/RAF	**MJ460**	3W-N	†
	F/O Coenraad **MANDERS**	RAF No. 113889	(NL)/RAF	**MK208**	3W-R	-
			SPITFIRE Mk XVI			
28.01.45	F/Sgt Cornelis **KOOY**	RAF No. 1814967	(NL)/RAF	**RK840**	3W-M	†
13.02.45	F/O Eric **DITMARSH**	RAF No. 173037	(NL)/RAF	**RK892**	3W-A	†
	F/Sgt Adriaan **BARY**	RAF No. 1649905	(NL)/RAF	**RK921**	3W-F	PoW
14.02.45	F/O Frans **VAN EIJK**	RAF No. 113894	(NL)/RAF	**RK895**	3W-E	†
24.02.45	F/L Rudolf **VAN DAALEN WETTERS**	RAF No. 104590	(NL)/RAF	**TB339**	3W-E	-
25.02.45	F/O Pieter **CRAMERUS**	RAF No. 143220	(NL)/RAF	**TB331**	3W-X	-
	Sgt Laurens **KNAPPERT**	RAF No. 1649976	(NL)/RAF	**TB494**	3W-C	-
05.03.45	F/O Johannes **VLUG**	RAF No. 145141	(NL)/RAF	**RR240**	3W-N	†
26.03.45	F/Sgt Tony **BIALLOSTERSKI**	RAF No. 1814922	(NL)/RAF	**PV288**	3W-J	-
30.03.45	W/O Hendrik **CRAMM**	RAF No. 1692491	(NL)/RAF	**RK891**	3W-T	†
	F/Sgt Ronald E. **JESS**	RAF No. 1585023	RAF	**TB478**	3W-F	-
01.04.45	P/O Martin **JANSSEN**	RAF No. 195197	(NL)/RAF	**RK897**	3W-L	Inj.
	F/O Leonard **HENDRIKX**	*n/k*	(NL)/RAF	**RK883**	3W-B	Inj.

Date	Pilot	S/N	Origin	Serial	Code	Fate
	W/O Johannes **van Roosendaal**	RAF No. 1692496	(NL)/RAF	**TB907**	3W-E	**Eva.**
	F/O Aart **Homburg**	RAF No. 125169	(NL)/RAF	**RR249**	3W-Y	†
16.04.45	F/Sgt Gerard **Dijkman**	RAF No. 1814946	(NL)/RAF	**TD115**	3W-Q	-
17.04.45	F/Sgt Marin **Rackwitz**	RAF No. 1814902	(NL)/RAF	**TB997**	3W-H	-
22.04.45	F/Sgt Servaas **Aertsen**	RAF No. 1814930	(NL)/RAF	**TD157**	3W-G	-
23.04.45	F/O Kenneth **Norman**	RAF No. 148549	RAF	**TB627**	3W-U	†

Total: 31

Flak remained the main danger for the Allied fighter-bombers until the end of war. Very accurate, Flak caused considerable damages to aircraft. This Dutch pilot is watching the Flak damages located near the cockpit. He got luck this time!

Summary of the aircraft lost by accident - 322 Squadron

Date	Pilot	S/N	Origin	Serial	Code	Fate
				Spitfire Mk V		
25.11.43	Sgt Martin **Janssen**	RAF No. 1814942	(NL)/RAF	**BL715**	VL-F	-
16.01.44	F/O Gilles **de Neve**	RAF No. 113891	(NL)/RAF	**AD428**		†
				Spitfire Mk XIV		
11.04.44	F/O Jakob **van Hamel**	RAF No. 132085	(NL)/RAF	**NH700**	VL-P	†
				Spitfire Mk IX		
09.08.44	P/O Aart **Homburg**	RAF No. 125169	(NL)/RAF	**MJ243**		-
				Spitfire Mk XVI		
03.02.45	F/O Johannes **Koes**	RAF No. 145139	(NL)/RAF	**RK865**		†
19.03.45	F/Sgt Saul D. **Lazarus**	RAF No. 1437557	RAF	**RR205**		†
08.05.45	F/L Donald J. **Hunter**	RAF No. 150142	(US)/RAF	**TB383**		†
	W/O Johannes **van Roosendaal**	RAF No. 1692496	(NL)/RAF	**TD131**		-
24.07.45	F/Sgt Tony **Biallosterski**	RAF No. 1814922	(NL)/RAF	**RK906**		-

Total: 9

Supermarine Spitfire Mk.VB BM354
No. 322 (Dutch) Squadron
Hornchurch (UK), autumn 1943

Supermarine Spitfire Mk.IX MJ360
No. 322 (Dutch) Squadron
Deanland (UK), September 1944

Supermarine Spitfire Mk XIV NH699
No. 322 (Dutch) Squadron
Dealand (UK), August 1944

NB: No D-Day stripes were painted on this aircraft, profile made from a wartime footage

Victories - confirmed or probable claims: -

First operational sortie:
20.05.44
Last operational sortie:
30.10.45

Number of sorties: *ca.*950

Total aircraft written-off:
22

Aircraft lost on operations: 14
Aircraft lost in accidents: 8

Squadron code letters:

-

COMMANDING OFFICERS			
Maj Hans MAURENBRECHER	NEIAF	10.12.43	29.07.45
Maj Harry SIMONS	NEIAF	29.07.45	15.07.45
Maj Hans MAURENBRECHER	NEIAF	15.07.45	...

SQUADRON USAGE

The Dutch connection with the Curtiss P-40 started as early as the Japanese invasion of the Netherlands East Indies during late 1941/early 1942. As reinforcements, the Americans sent the 17th Pursuit Squadron, equipped with P-40Es, in January 1943 while more reinforcements were on the way, with some P-40s being allocated to the Dutch or the RAF. Indeed, as far as the Dutch were concerned, 36 aircraft had been requested under Requisition N-122 on 10 February 1942. A convoy left Perth, Australia, for Java on 22 February; while some P-40s managed to reach their destination, only three were made available for flight testing on 7 March. They never flew and Java surrendered soon after. While some P-40s were destroyed before the surrender, others were captured intact, or almost intact, and repaired by the Japanese. Requisition N-122 was logically cancelled in April.

The Dutch air schools had had time to evacuate to Australia, continuing their travel to the USA where a Dutch flying school was formed at Jackson Army Air Base in Mississippi in the late spring of 1942. Training soon resumed; included in the courses were some P-40s for the latter stages of training. Nine P-40Ns were requested as trainers for the NEIAF and eventually delivered in May 1943; they all returned to the USAAF in February 1944 when the last class graduated. In the meantime, and under Requisition N-511, the NEIAF obtained 67 more P-40Ns to be used in Australia; they received the serials C3-500 to C3-566 and were delivered between November 1943 and November 1944. The production blocks were split as 34 P-40N-20-CUs, 15 N-25-CUs, 6 N-30-CUs and 12 N-35-CUs which differed with minor changes and equipment. These aircraft were destined to form a fighter squadron plus reserves under RAAF authority. At the end of Summer 1943, enough progress had been made to consider sending 19 pilots and several instructors to Australia to form the nucleus of a fighter unit. This detachment was placed under the command of Major H.A. Maurenbrecher. They left on 1 October and arrived in Australia in the first week of November. To familiarise with RAAF procedures, the Dutch pilots were sent to Mildura and No. 2 Operational Training Unit.

On 10 December, No. 120 (NEI) Squadron was officially formed at Canberra as a fighter squadron. The first aircraft were collected on 31 and 31 December 1943 and, by 22 January, the unit had received its full complement of aircraft and was at a strength of 213 RAAF officers and airmen, with 28 officers and airmen of the NEIAF. Indeed, while the flying personnel was Dutch, there was not enough Dutch groundcrew so, as with No. 18 (NEI) Squadron flying Mitchells, the RAAF had to provide its own personnel.

The original plans were for 120 to operate alongside 18 (NEI) in the Northern Territory. This did not eventuate; the decision was made for the unit to operate from Merauke in Dutch New Guinea instead. However, the deployment was delayed due to a perceived Japanese invasion threat in Western Australia during March 1944. By 27 March, the threat had disappeared and 120 was ordered back across the country to Canberra via Potshot–Forrest–Kalgoorlie–Ceduna. Two unserviceable planes followed the next day, flown by Lt A. Geerts and Sgt J. Brameyer, but they got lost and were obliged to bale out when they ran out of fuel. Geerts landed badly and broke his ankle. It was a bad start for the squadron. On 31 March, the decision was made to move from Canberra to Merauke where it would replace No. 86 Squadron RAAF (also flying P-40s). The advance party departed on 10 April, travelling in

Born in Java in the Netherlands East Indies (NEI), Hans Maurenbrecher enlisted in the Royal Netherlands Army in the NEI in 1932 to become a regular officer. By 1939, he switched to the newly formed ML-KNIL, the air force of the NEI, and, when war broke out in the Pacific, he had reached the rank of captain and was a test pilot for the Brewster 339 Buffalo fighters the ML-KNIL had purchased. Having been repatriated to Australia after the fall of the NEI, he was sent to Jackson, Mississippi, where Dutch personnel from the NEI were trained, and became a flight instructor. At the end of 1943, he was given command of the new No. 120 (NEI) Squadron which became operational from March 1944 over the south-west Pacific. Maurenbrecher remained at the head of 120 beyond the cessation of hostilities.

After the end of the war, he remained in the ML-KNIL and, when independence was granted to the NEI, continued his career in the Netherlands until retiring in 1963 as a Lieutenant-General.

Curtiss P-40N-20-CU C3-500
No. 120 (NEI) Squadron
Major H. Maurenbrecher
Merauke (New Guinea), summer 1944

Curtiss P-40N-35-CU C3-560
No. 120 (NEI) Squadron
Major H. Maurenbrecher
Biak (New Guinea), 1945-1946

P-40 C3-526 being serviced at Merauke in 1944.

three Dakotas and a Mitchell. The main party arrived in Sydney by train on 27 April where they embarked for passage to Merauke, eventually arriving on 9 May after the aircraft had been ferried from Canberra. Intensive training of all kinds (aerial tactics, gunnery, dive bombing and air combat) was carried out in May and the first operational sorties, a simple patrol, were flown on the 20th by Lieutenants H. Simons (C3-526) and J. Verspoor (C3-508). On the 26th, a scramble was ordered to identify a plane which proved to be friendly and, the next day, four P-40s got airborne to search for a missing C-47. In June, the main activity remained the interception of various unidentified aircraft which all proved to be friendly. A change came on the 27th when the first offensive sortie was carried out, an armed recce of Cooke Bay led by Major Maurenbrecher; owing to a low ceiling and poor visibility, no results were observed.

On 4 July, a section of four aircraft led by Capt Mulder made a bombing and strafing attack at Japero; it was the first attack made by 120, but the results were unobserved. The next day, the mission was repeated but Lt J. Verspoor suffered a fuel leak and was forced to make a forced landing ten miles south of Cook Bay. Wireless communications were maintained for a period after the aircraft crash landed on a beach. By arrangement with No. 12 Squadron RAAF, supplies were dropped by two Vultee Vengeances; one package reached its mark, the others being lost in the scrub and the sea. Verspoor was eventually rescued by a Catalina the next day and the P-40 destroyed by gunfire. It was certainly a rather chaotic start as two incidents then took place within two days, damaging two P-40s, C3-520 and 540, the latter being eventually written off. While there was no human cost, both aircraft were grounded for a while. Less fortunate was Sgt R. Pelsmaker who was killed in a practice flight south of Nassam village on the 25th. On 28 July, Sgt R. Spoor lost control of C3-510 when he taxied at too high a speed and ended up in a ditch; yet another aircraft had to leave the squadron for repairs. While over 60 sorties were flown in July, this was doubled in July. No major event was noted expect on the 24th when, during a scramble, 2Lt N. Czismazia de Somogy was informed by another aircraft, ten minutes after take-off, that his engine was on fire. He baled out safely three miles north-east of the Merauke strip. A few days later, another P-40, C3-530, was sent for repairs after another beach landing following an engine failure. The bad news continued as misfortune hit the squadron heavily on 6 September. Ten pilots of the first group were relieved; seven were selected to fly as passengers on a Dakota while the other three were ordered to ferry C3-505, 513 and 522 to NEI Personnel and Equipment Pool (PEP) in Canberra. The Dakota, DT-941, was seen to take off but it was later posted missing. Among the 20 fatalities were the seven 120 Squadron pilots: 1Lts R. Braakensiek, H. Levy and J. Zwart (all patrol leaders), 1Lts B. van Aken, O. Leyding and R. Salm, and Sgt A. Scholte. September's carnage was not yet over as 120 lost two P-40s in a collision on the 19th. During a patrol following a scramble, Sgt G. van Aphen passed out through lack of oxygen and perished while his wingman, 1Lt W. Heikoop (ex-18 Squadron NEI), parachuted to safety. At the same time, S/Maj F. Verdier, the third pilot of the patrol, forced landed on a beach 35 miles from Merauke owing to an electrical failure. The P-40 could not be salvaged as some trees had snapped the wings off and the fuselage was badly damaged. On 2 October, C3-533, piloted by Lt M. Soesman, caught fire at 19,000 feet. The pilot switched off his engine and made a dead-stick landing on the strip, saving the aircraft. While two more incidents were recorded in October, Soesman's adventure remained the main event of the month which saw operational activity drop to about 40 sorties. This reduced further to 26 in November. Two more P-40s were wrecked, however: C3-506 crashed at the end of the runway on return from a strike on the 16th following a flap failure. Three days later, Capt Mulder was killed when he stalled following the pull out on the bombing range. Another pilot was posted missing on 7 December; Lt Sandberg failed to return after taking off for Tanah Merah in a CAC Wirraway. His luck stayed with him, however, as he was found safe a few days later. Several days after his recovery, three pilots were detached to No. 80 Squadron RAAF to gain operational experience but Lt P.de Jager would never return; he was killed in action in C3-554 on the 10th during an attack on an enemy steamer off Lantor Island.

At the end of 1944, the future location of the squadron was in doubt due to the redeployment of RAAF units from Merauke. After much planning, the squadron was scheduled to move to Jacquinot Bay, New Britain. Therefore, operational flying was almost non-existent during January and February 1945. On 13 February, the squadron became non-operational in preparation for the move. However, an accident before the move took place the following day when Lt F. de Raadt crashed on take-off from Tanah Merah on the 7th; the P-40 was only good for spare parts. Three days later, Lt C. Been crashed C3-533 in New South Wales while ferrying the aircraft to the NEI PEP for modifications, which, of course, were cancelled! The eventual move ended up taking a lot of time. Ready by 1 March, the ship earmarked for the move only arrived on the 12th and sailed into Jacquinot Bay on 9 May; that day, however, the destination was announced as Mokmer Airfield on Biak. On 16 May, 15 pilots went to Canberra to attend a refresher course. They were back on the 27th.

The first echelon arrived at Biak on 17 May and the first pilots arrived direct from Merauke on 1 June. Within a week, 120 was complete and ready for action once more. On 12 June, led by Major Maurenbrecher, ten P-40s attacked fuel dumps and a troop concentration west of Moemi strip. During the month, eight strikes were made in the Vogelkop and Geelvink Bay areas where the pilots used glide-bombing techniques which impressed with their accuracy. Other targets were barges and any marine craft, and photographic reconnaissance missions were undertaken over Mansin Island. In all, 58 sorties were flown in June. In July, this figure passed 170, with a first loss recorded on the 9th when *Luitenant-ter-zee* R. Idzerda of the Royal Dutch Navy failed to return from a strafing sortie on barracks near Manokwari area; hit by ground fire he bailed out and was rescued soon after. But some operational changes occurred on the 16th when the squadron was placed under the newly activated No. 11 Group RAAF with three tasks: local defence and patrolling sea lanes and land routes; support of ground forces and attacks against enemy targets; and communication flights. An additional task was making photo flights. On 19 July, in concert with 12 Beauforts of No. 15 Squadron RAAF, the Dutch bombed and strafed Sijara, Saborwa and Foemoe. Officer Cadet Esser who had joined early in the month was hit in the engine by ground fire and ditched off Doom Island. Lieutenant G. Fokkinga circled the crash for 15 minutes as top cover and was relieved by Australian Beauforts. After four days, the unfortunate pilot was eventually rescued and back with his squadron. During the same op in which Essler was shot down, 1Lt W. Heikoop was also hit by flak over Sorong but managed to land at Middleburg where he crashed his P-40. Later that fateful day, 2Lt F. Braun had his undercarriage collapse before taking off; the P-40 was damaged. On

P-40N C3-503 'Wham Bam!' at Merauke in 1944. *(Collections Nederlands Instituut voor Militaire Historie - NIMH)*

B Flight pilots a Merauke in 1944:
Standing on the wing L-R, 2Lt W. van Nuts, Sgt T. Gottschalk, 2Lt H. Levy, 2Lt J. Flemer, 1Lt P. Stam, 2Lt de Smalen.
On the nose, 2Lt R. Braakensiek, 2Lt M. Soesman, 2Lt J. Hoekstra, Sgt G. Greene, Capt Y. Mulder.
Sitting on the leading edge of the wing, 2Lt F. de Raadt, 1Lt C. Been, Cpl H Haye , 2Lt R. Trebels and standing on the ground, Officer Cadet Hmelnitsky (IO).
(Collections Nederlands Instituut voor Militaire Historie - NIMH)

29 July, Major Maurenbrecher departed for NEI HQ and was replaced by Capt H. Simons who became the acting CO and was promoted to major (Maurenbrecher would be back on 15 September). Attacks on the Manokwari area continued during the first week of August during which 58 sorties were carried out. The heaviest day was the 1st. The squadron was tasked to participate in the attack on the Manokwari radio beacon. This Japanese installation transmitted on the same frequency as the Biak radio beacon, causing unwary pilots to home on the wrong beacon in bad weather, receiving an unexpected dose of AAA as a welcome; it had to be destroyed. At around 10.00, 15 P-40Ns arrived overhead the target, each armed with two 500-lb bombs. Their mission was to neutralise the AA defenses allowing the Beauforts of 15 Squadron to attack the target with heavier bombs. The attack consisted of dive bombing from 12,000 feet, followed by a strafing run from the land side towards the sea. This way a pilot could have a chance to bale out over the sea to be rescued. But things went wrong; in just a few minutes, the Dutch sustained their heaviest losses since the formation of the squadron. Lieutenant Fokkinga had a bomb hang up and received two hits in the engine, causing it to stop. His first impulse was to open his canopy and jump but he decided to try to ditch despite the risk of the bomb exploding or the plane turning upside down. He successfully made his landing, managed to get into his dinghy and was rescued within two hours. Sergeant F. Hirdes of the Royal Dutch Navy was less fortunate and was shot down and killed while Sgt W. Bakhuys-Roozebaum also managed a safe ditching and was rescued after five hours. Four other P-40Ns were damaged, three of them heading directly to Noemfoor for repairs while 2Lt J. Scheffer made a belly landing at Mokmer with a hydraulic failure. A few days later, the first atomic bomb was dropped, followed by the second on the 9th, meaning the end of the war was near. Operations had to continue, however, and sorties were flown until the 17th when a reconnaissance flight led by Major Simons over Manokwari was made, the squadron's final operation. Sadly, it had previously lost its last pilot on the 11th when Lt J. van Olmen was shot down in flames by AAA south a Manokwari while strafing enemy positions in the Ransiki–Moemi area. By mid-August, where operational flying had halted, the squadron was using C3-500, 501, 509, 510, 518, 525, 531, 536, 549, 552, 555, 556, 558, 560, 562, 563, 564 and 565 (C3-561 arrived soon after to replace C3-541 lost on the 11th).

During September and October 1945, under the command of Major Maurenbrecher, who had resumed command, 120 carried out surveillance flights (64 in two months), provided air cover for various purposes, searched for barges and dropped leaflets. However, during October, the possible move of the NEI squadrons to Java put the question of the future of the unit's RAAF members in doubt. Subsequently, the RAAF elements of the NEI squadrons were disbanded on the field on 30 October, but it was not until February 1946 that all were posted out from the squadron. On 20 June 1946, 120 Squadron came under the operational control of the NEI Army Air Headquarters where it would begin a new mission.

Ground crew at Mokmer, Biak, preparing C3-549/H for the next op. The tail letter was applied in 1945. *(AHM of WA)*

A sequence showing a typical mission assigned to 120: a patrol of four P 40Ns (aircraft 'E', 'H', 'Q' and 'Y') flying off the New Guinea coast loaded with two 250-lb bombs. The aircraft visible are C3 526/H 'Snafu', C3 500/Y and C3 534/E. The first photo on the previous page shows aircraft 'Q' and 'E' taxiing for the runway.
(Collections Nederlands Instituut voor Militaire Historie - NIMH)

A P 40N on standby near the operations tent. *(AHM of WA)*

Date	Pilot	S/N	Origin	Serial	Code	Fate
05.07.44	2Lt Julles VERSPOOR		NEIAF	**C3-515**		-
24.08.44	2Lt Nicolaas CZISMARIA DE S.		NEIAF	**C3-508**		-
19.09.44	1Lt Willem HEIKOOP		NEIAF	**C3-544**		-
	Sgt Gijs VAN ALPHEN		NEIAF	**C3-503**		†
	S/Maj F. VERDIER	91952	NEIAF	**C3-550**		-
16.11.44	1Lt Jan STRUIK		NEIAF	**C3-506**		†
10.12.44	1Lt Paul DE JAGER		NEAIF	**C3-554**		†
09.07.45	Ltz2 Ruud IDZERDA		RNethN	**C3-528**		-
19.07.45	1Lt Willem HEIKOOP		NEIAF	**C3-546**		-
	Vdg ESSER		NEIAF	**C3-557**		-
01.08.45	1Lt Gerard FOKKINGA		NEIAF	**C3-562**		-
	Sgt F. HIRDES	21148	RNethN	**C3-534**		†
	Sgt Willem BAKHUYS-ROOZEBOOM		NEIAF	**C3-504**		-
11.08.45	1Lt Johannes VAN OLMEN		NEIAF	**C3-541**		†

Total: 14

N.B. The following P-40s were written off or struck of charge for unrecorded reasons while located at Marauke or Biak, possibly after an operational mishap: C3-526, C3-539, C3-545

Date	Pilot	S/N	Origin	Serial	Code	Fate
29.03.44	2Lt Arjen **Geerts**		NEIAF	**C3-527**		-
	Sgt Jan **Brameyer**	93089	NEIAF	**C3-524**		-
07.07.44	2Lt Nicolaas **Czismaria de S.**		NEIAF	**C3-540**		-
25.07.44	Sgt Rudolf **Pelsmaker**	49232	NEIAF	**C3-514**		†
30.08.44	Sgt Hugo **Haye**	34824	NEAIF	**C3-530**		-
19.11.44	Capt Y.H. **Mulder**		NEAIF	**C3-553**		†
07.02.45	1Lt Frederik **de Raadt**		NEAIF	**C3-542**		-
17.02.45	1Lt C. **Been**		NEAIF	**C3-533**		-

Total: 8

N.B. The following P-40s were also lost in various accident while based in Australia, most of the time on training sorties: C3-512, C3-513, C3-517, C3-519, C3-535, C3-543, C3-566. Of the 67 P-40s supplied to the Dutch, 35 survived the war.

DUTCH P-40 REGISTER

Serials	Formerly	Block	Postwar J-serial
C3-500	43-22972	P-40N-20-CU	J-300
C3-501	43-22974	P-40N-20-CU	J-301
C3-502	43-22975	P-40N-20-CU	J-302
C3-503	43-22976	P-40N-20-CU	-
C3-504	43-22977	P-40N-20-CU	-
C3-505	43-22978	P-40N-20-CU	-
C3-506	43-22979	P-40N-20-CU	-
C3-507	43-22980	P-40N-20-CU	J-307
C3-508	43-22981	P-40N-20-CU	-
C3-509	43-22982	P-40N-20-CU	J-309
C3-510	43-22983	P-40N-20-CU	-
C3-511	43-22984	P-40N-20-CU	J-311
C3-512	43-22789	P-40N-20-CU	-
C3-513	43-22790	P-40N-20-CU	-
C3-514	43-22793	P-40N-20-CU	-
C3-515	43-22799	P-40N-20-CU	-
C3-516	43-22762	P-40N-20-CU	J-316
C3-517	43-22763	P-40N-20-CU	-
C3-518	43-22769	P-40N-20-CU	J-318
C3-519	43-22771	P-40N-20-CU	-
C3-520	43-22772	P-40N-20-CU	J-320
C3-521	43-22774	P-40N-20-CU	-
C3-522	43-22775	P-40N-20-CU	J-322
C3-523	43-22777	P-40N-20-CU	-
C3-524	43-22778	P-40N-20-CU	-

C3-525	43-22784	P-40N-20-CU	-
C3-526	43-22804	P-40N-20-CU	-
C3-527	43-22757	P-40N-20-CU	-
C3-528	43-22985	P-40N-20-CU	-
C3-529	43-22986	P-40N-20-CU	J-329
C3-530	43-22988	P-40N-20-CU	-
C3-531	43-22991	P-40N-20-CU	J-331
C3-532	43-22995	P-40N-20-CU	J-332
C3-533	43-23003	P-40N-20-CU	-
C3-534	43-24347	P-40N-25-CU	-
C3-535	43-24379	P-40N-25-CU	-
C3-536	43-24353	P-40N-25-CU	-
C3-537	43-24355	P-40N-25-CU	J-337
C3-538	43-24357	P-40N-25-CU	-
C3-539	43-24537	P-40N-25-CU	-
C3-540	43-24540	P-40N-25-CU	-
C3-541	43-24541	P-40N-25-CU	-
C3-542	43-24545	P-40N-25-CU	-
C3-543	43-24549	P-40N-25-CU	-
C3-544	43-24548	P-40N-25-CU	-
C3-545	43-24552	P-40N-25-CU	-
C3-546	43-24553	P-40N-25-CU	-
C3-547	43-24556	P-40N-25-CU	J-347
C3-548	43-24544	P-40N-25-CU	-
C3-549	44-7195	P-40N-30-CU	J-349
C3-550	44-7198	P-40N-30-CU	-
C3-551	44-7200	P-40N-30-CU	J-351
C3-552	44-7202	P-40N-30-CU	J-352
C3-553	44-7207	P-40N-30-CU	-
C3-554	44-7209	P-40N-30-CU	-
C3-555	44-7856	P-40N-35-CU	J-355
C3-556	44-7857	P-40N-35-CU	J-356
C3-557	44-7858	P-40N-35-CU	-
C3-558	44-7859	P-40N-35-CU	J-358
C3-559	44-7860	P-40N-35-CU	J-359
C3-560	44-7861	P-40N-35-CU	J-360
C3-561	44-7862	P-40N-35-CU	-
C3-562	44-7863	P-40N-35-CU	-
C3-563	44-7864	P-40N-35-CU	-
C3-564	44-7865	P-40N-35-CU	-
C3-565	44-7866	P-40N-35-CU	J-365
C3-566	44-7867	P-40N-35-CU	-

C3-502/B and C3-503 'Wham Bam!' warming up their engine at Mearake in 1944.

SQUADRONS! - The series

Donald James Matthew BLAKESLEE DFC

Supermarine Spitfire Mk.VB EN951
No. 133 (Eagle) Squadron
Flight Lieutenant D. J. M. Blakeslee
CAN./ J.4351
Gravesend (UK), August 1942

Charles Cuthbertson LEARMONTH DFC*

Douglas Boston Mk. III A28-9 (ex-AL691)
No. 22 Squadron RAAF
Squadron Leader C. C. Learmonth
A29-383
Port Moresby (New Guinea), spring 1943

Hans Anton MAURENBRECHER

Curtiss P-40N-35-CU C3-560
No. 120 (NEI) Squadron
Major H. Maurenbrecher
Biak (New Guinea), 1943-1946

Roland Prosper BEAMONT DSO* DFC*

Hawker Tempest Mk.V JN751
No. 150 Wing
Wing Commander R. P. Beamont
RAF No. 41819
Bradwell Bay (UK), April 1944

Ronald Thomas SUSANS DSO DFC

North American P-51D-25-NT A68-724
No. 77 squadron, RAAF
Squadron Leader R. T. Susans
O4391
Bofu (Japan), 1947

James Henry LACEY DFM*

Supermarine Spitfire Mk.XIV RN135
No. 17 Squadron
Squadron Leader J. H. Lacey
RAF No. 112708
Seletar (Singapore), autumn 1945

Introducing's RAF In Combat and Bravo Bravo Aviation's collection of
highly-detailed and historically accurate, high-quality aviation prints.
For more information on available prints, please visit :

WWW.RAF-IN-COMBAT.com   or

Bram van der STOK

Supermarine Spitfire Mk.XVI TD137
No. 322 (Dutch) Squadron
Squadron Leader B. van der Stok
RAF No. 106346
B.116/Wünsdorf (Germany), summer 1945

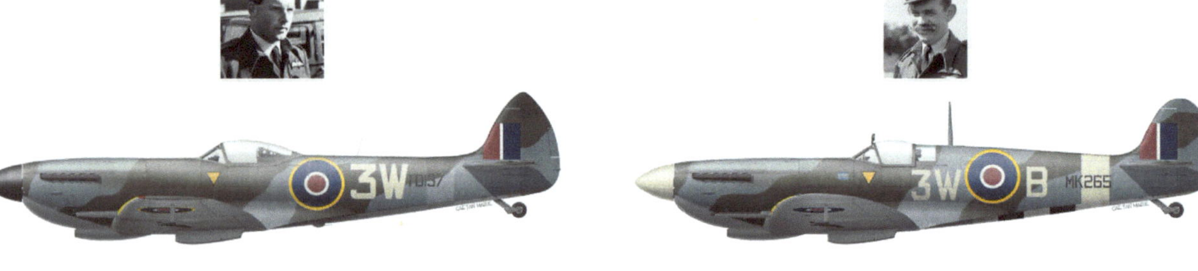

Leendert Carel Marie van EENDENBURG

Supermarine Spitfire Mk.IX MK265
No. 322 (Dutch) Squadron
Squadron Leader L. van Eendenburg
RAF No. 108814
Hawkinge (UK), September 1944

Keith Cowie KUHLMANN DFC

Supermarine Spitfire Mk.XIV NH718
No. 322 (Dutch) Squadron
Major K. C. Kuhlmann (SAAF)
SAAF No. P102441V
West Malling (UK), June-July 1944

Prints available for this book:

PL-002: K.C. Kuhlmann
PL-049: J. Plesman
PL-089: A.C. Stewart
PL-090: B. Van der Stock
PL-091: L. van Eendenburg
PL-092: H. Maurenbrecher
PL-093: H. Maurenbrecher (2)
PL-296: J. Plesman (2)